THE GROWTH AND INFLUENCE OF CLASSICAL GREEK POETRY

LECTURES DELIVERED IN 1892 ON THE PERCY TURNBULL MEMORIAL FOUNDATION IN THE JOHNS HOPKINS UNIVERSITY

BY

R. C. JEBB

REGIUS PROFESSOR OF GREEK IN THE UNIVERSITY OF CAMBRIDGE

GORDIAN PRESS
NEW YORK
1970

Originally Published 1893
Reprinted 1970

Library of Congress Catalog Card Number—79-93247
Standard Book Number—87752-054-2
Published by GORDIAN PRESS, INC.

To

DANIEL C. GILMAN, LL. D.

PRESIDENT OF THE JOHNS HOPKINS UNIVERSITY,

𝕮𝖍𝖎𝖘 𝖁𝖔𝖑𝖚𝖒𝖊,

WHICH OWES ITS EXISTENCE TO HIS FRIENDSHIP,

IS AFFECTIONATELY DEDICATED.

PREFACE.

THE Percy Turnbull Memorial Lectureship of
Poetry was established in the Johns Hopkins
University, Baltimore, in 1889, by Mr. and Mrs.
Lawrence Turnbull, in memory of their son, Percy
Graeme Turnbull. The first course was given
in 1891, by Mr. Edmund Clarence Stedman, on
"The Nature and Elements of Poetry," and was
followed, in 1892, by the course contained in this
volume.

The lectures are printed as they were delivered,
with the exception of a few very slight changes.
Their aim is to exhibit concisely, but clearly, the
leading characteristics of the best classical Greek
poets, and to illustrate the place of ancient Greece
in the general history of poetry. I should like the
book to be considered as a member of a series, to
which other volumes, by other writers, will doubtless, in due course, be added; a series deriving
unity from the Turnbull foundation, and associated with the University, whose place among
elder sisters is already one of such peculiar distinction.

As these pages will meet the eyes of some among those who heard the lectures given, I may be allowed to renew here the expression of my warm gratitude to that audience at Baltimore whose sympathy, so encouraging at the time, will always be to me one of the brightest of memories.

R. C. JEBB.

CONTENTS.

I.

III.

GREEK EPIC POETRY (*continued*).

IV.

V.

PINDAR.

VI.

THE ATTIC DRAMA.

THE GROWTH AND INFLUENCE
OF CLASSICAL GREEK
POETRY

THE

GROWTH AND INFLUENCE OF CLASSICAL GREEK POETRY

I

THE DISTINCTIVE QUALITIES OF THE GREEK RACE AS EXPRESSED BY HOMER

THE literature of Europe begins with the Homeric poems. That very fact tends to obscure our appreciation of them. They are the sources of a stream which has descended to these days, through many channels, indeed, but with a continuous course. We compare the Iliad with the Aeneid or with Paradise Lost; the Greek genius with the Roman, the Celtic, or the Teutonic, — and recognize, in these relations, the qualities distinctive of the Hellene. But no such process can convey an adequate idea of the significance that Homeric poetry possessed for the world in which it first appeared. It is needful also to remember what had been the general tendencies of ancient civilization down to the age in which that poetry took its rise. The Hellenic race, and its first intellectual product, must be seen against this

The Hellenic mind — a novel force in the ancient world.

background, before its originality can be fully apprehended.

In the tenth century before Christ, epic com-

The pre-
hellenic
civilizations. position, of the mature type found in the Iliad and the Odyssey, had already been developed by the Greeks. No one acquainted with the results of recent criticism will hold, I think, that this date is too early. Let us take the tenth century, then, as an approximate epoch, and consider what was, at that period, the general state of intellectual development in the foremost civilizations of the ancient world. The survey must be brief and slight; but, if we wish to appreciate the Hellenes, a little space may be usefully bestowed on defining these standards of comparison.

When that tenth century opened, the civilization

Egypt in the
tenth century
B. C. of Egypt was, at the least, between two and three thousand years old. The Egyptian state rested upon two closely connected foundations; first, a hierarchy of officials, — at its head, the king, exalted above human rank, Pharaoh, the descendant of the god Ra, and the intercessor between gods and men; secondly, a religion which dominated every part of life, and in which the central point was the care for the dead. Those mighty monuments, the greatest ever reared by man, with which Egyptian history begins, show these two elements combined. There we see how the king exerted the whole power of the state, all its wealth and all its re-

sources of labor, to make a splendid and inde-
structible mansion for his corpse, — the everlasting house in which his immortal double, his Ka,
should dwell when it had quitted the temporary
abodes of the living. Every Egyptian, according
to his rank and the means at his disposal, strove
for the same object. How intensely real the Ka,
the immortal double, was to the Egyptian, may be
seen by an example which M. Maspèro has cited.
The scribe Qeni was haunted for months by the
spirit (Ka) of his wife Onkhari. He had always
treated her well while she was in the world, had
given her an expensive funeral, and left her a considerable income; yet she was angry with him,
and continually returned to disturb him. He
could only free himself from the annoyance by
threatening her with a legal action. He wrote to
her, asking the reason of her posthumous rage,
and reminding her of all the affection that he had
shown her. "Since I became thy husband until
this day, what have I done against thee that I
should hide? What wilt thou do when I am
obliged to bear witness as to my treatment of
thee, when I appear with thee before the tribunal
of Osiris, to plead my own cause before the gods
of the West, and thou wilt be judged according to
this writing, which will contain my complaints
against thee. What wilt thou do?" The roll of
papyrus, attached to a wooden statuette of the woman, and placed in the tomb, reached its address;
and Onkhari, fearing to be called in judgment before Osiris, ceased to trouble.

Before the close of the sixteenth century B. C.,
— so Egyptologists tell us, — everything in the
Egyptian cultus had become stereotyped. Every
hymn, every temple inscription, had come to be
composed after a fixed pattern. The minutest
details of ritual had been formulated in writing.
A canonical book regulated the daily occupations
of the king. Geometry, astronomy, medicine —
indeed, all Egyptian knowledge — had been di-
gested into sacred treatises. The very life after
death had been mapped out; the priests knew
what demons guarded what gates of the other
world, and what incantations must be used in each
case. Thus the shadow of superstition fell upon
the entire existence of the Egyptian. His constant anxiety was to do that which was of good
omen, and to avoid the contrary. The priesthood,
with its monopoly of sacred wisdom, grew stronger
and stronger. Religion became not only the principal, but almost the sole, concern of the state.
The priests controlled the king; at last a priest
seized the throne, and a priestly dynasty was
founded. Next in importance to the priests, at
the epoch roughly marked by the tenth century,
were the soldiers. The Egypt of 1000 B. C., it has
been said, differed from that of 1500 years earlier
as widely as the military empire of the First Napo-
leon differed from the France of St. Louis. The
mental stamina of the people had been enfeebled
by the despotism of an all-engrossing ritual. Religion was no longer the mainstay of patriotism,

but had usurped the place of patriotism itself. As for literature, it had always in Egypt been restricted to the priesthood and the official class. It had consisted chiefly of religious texts, state records, or biographical memoirs, with some fables or stories. But here, too, the deadening influence of stereotyped formulas had prevailed. The age which saw the birth of Homeric epos found Egypt with her material civilization highly developed, but stricken with intellectual barrenness, and without any vigorous pulse of national existence. The life of the state and of the individual had been crushed by the weight of sacerdotal tradition.

A different form of despotism brooded over the lands of the Euphrates and the Tigris. Babylonia In the tenth century B. C. two great and Assyria. monarchies there stood side by side. The elder, Babylonia, had been the teacher of the other in religion, in material civilization, in science, art, and literature. The Assyrians were essentially warriors ; and their relations to their Babylonian neighbors were, in some points, not unlike those of the Romans to the Greeks. In the religion of Babylonia, on which that of Assyria was founded, a potent element was the fear of evil demons. The world was believed to be full of such malignant beings, ever on the watch for men, as they leave or enter their houses, at their meals, in their hours of rest, — in all their movements and actions. Fancy invested these beings with the

most grotesque and horrible shapes that a disor-
dered imagination could conceive ; such shapes as
might haunt a sick man's troubled dreams, shapes
in which the human form was blended with that
of animals, or those of animals with each other.
Thus the goddess of the gloomy under-world, she
whom they called Allat, had a human trunk with
a lion's head, and the wings and claws of a bird of
prey ; each of her hands was armed with a large
serpent, which she brandished like a living javelin.
The demons, her servants, were composite monsters of a like kind.   The gods of the Babylonian
and Assyrian formed a divine army to protect him
against such demons, which were ever swarming,
invisible, around him ; and, as in an army, each
god had his appointed station ; one at the door of
the house, another on the roof, another at the table
or the bed.   The offerings made to the gods were
rewards for giving such protection.   Yet, vivid as
is the sense of the supernatural which such beliefs
indicate, there was a wide difference here between
Egypt and Babylonia.   The Babylonian religion
seems to have stopped short at a primitive stage.
It never became a paramount influence on the
spiritual and intellectual life of the people.   Where
men are penetrated by the conviction, not only
that there is an unending life after death, but
that the strict observance of certain precepts can
alone secure their happiness in that life, they will
yield unlimited obedience to the expounders of
such rules.   Hence the power of the Egyptian

priesthood. But the religion of Babylonia and Assyria did not conceive the life after death with any approach to Egyptian clearness and minute ness. There was a gloomy Hades, a place of tor ment ; and, for the virtuous, a place of happiness where the tree of life spreads its branches, and the river of life flows. There was, however, no doctrinal system which, as in Egypt, furnished the mortal with an accurate chart of the land beyond the grave, and with precise counsel for the preparation of his everlasting mansion. The sciences of astrology and magic were studied by the disciples of Chaldaean lore rather with a view to temporal welfare than with hopes transcending it. The royal astronomers, scanning the heavens from the tower of the Seven Planets, looked for signs presaging the king's victory in war, or his success in some other momentous enterprise ; the humble folk, whose traditional lore taught them something as to the language of the stars, consulted it for guidance in daily business or labor. Thus the priests, great as their influence was, never attained to that all-engrossing power which, like the process of petrifaction creeping over the form of Niobe, had slowly subdued the awe-stricken mind of Egypt. On this side of his existence, the Babylonian, and still more the warlike Assyrian, remained comparatively unfettered. But they, too, bore their yoke. The king of Babylonia and the king of Assyria were masters under whom the life of their subjects was, as the ancient Greeks thought, and as we should think, the life not of free men but of slaves. This thralldom was ordinarily borne, indeed, without complaint, or even with a loyal satisfaction ; but none the less did it preclude any high development of life, social or intellectual, so far, at least, as the vast majority of the people were concerned. In touching on this subject, it is well to remember that the data for Assyrian life in the seventh century B. C., in Assurbanipal's reign, cannot be assumed to hold good for a period 300 years earlier. Very little is known about the life of Assyria in 1000 B. C.; but the following statements may, I believe, be accepted. The traditional stores of knowledge, and the means of access to them, were confined, as in Egypt, to priests and officials. The great temples or the royal palaces contained the collections, open to priests and officials only, of brick tablets, stone plates, prisms, and cylinders, on which professional scribes had written the religious hymns, rituals, chronicles, state documents, treatises of astrology and mathematics. The early age of Chaldaea had produced some religious poems showing a real vigor of poetic imagination, — such as the descent of the goddess Ishtar (Astarte) into Hades, in search of the water of life which alone could restore her husband, the slain god Tammuz ; and the epic, if it may be so called, of the hero Isdubar, the lion-slayer, a Chaldaean Heracles. But no such poetical energy or freedom inspired the literary products of Assyria. The official scribes had no duty more important than to record the deeds of the monarch, the descendant of the god Assur, and the image of godhead upon earth ; nor is anything more suggestive, with regard to the level of Assyrian cultivation, than such records of the royal achievements. The great inscription of Tiglathpileser I., about 1120 B. C., is a typical example. In stereotyped phrases, which had come down from generation to generation, the conqueror boasts how he has destroyed hostile strongholds with fire and sword, how he has reduced multitudes to slavery, or put them to some appalling form of torture and death. Such chronicles, with their endless iterations, their dry annalistic manner, varied only by bombast, and their exultation in the most horrible cruelties, help us to conceive the condition of the Assyrians under autocrats who thus decorated the walls of their palaces. The sacerdotal despotism of Egypt, though deadening for the intellect, was at least penetrated by religious ideas ; it cannot have been so devoid of everything that avails to comfort or elevate the human spirit as was the royal despotism of Assyria.

Both these benumbing influences had been escaped by the Phoenicians, though their government was probably monarchical, *The Phoenicians.* and their priesthoods, probably hereditary, had great influence. In their career as the earliest traders and colonizers of the Mediterranean, — carrying the wares of the East to other lands, and planting factories or trading settlements where they went, — the Phoenicians showed a spirit of free enterprise unlike any that had yet appeared in the world. But its distinctive character is commercial. It was primarily associated with the pursuit of gain; it aimed at extended dominion as a means to the extension of trade. Phoenicians enlarged the boundaries of geographical knowledge; but that was merely an incident of voyages inspired by other motives than the spirit of exploration. It does not appear that the Phoenicians developed any intellectual activities beyond those — varied enough, doubtless — which were required in the manufacturer, the merchant, and the adventurous pioneer of commerce. Though often regarded by the ancients as great inventors, the Phoenicians do not seem to have possessed much real claim to originality. Their alphabet was probably derived from the Egyptian. The invention of arithmetic, and of systematic weights and measures, must be ascribed to the Babylonians. Glass-making, in which the Phoenicians excelled, was an art borrowed from Egypt. Their skill in embroidery, and in purple-dyeing, was again a double debt to Babylon. In their religion, the central point was the worship of the Sun, whose spouse was sometimes represented as the Earth, sometimes as the moon-goddess Astarte, the mother of the Tyrian sun-god Melkarth. They refrained from portraying their gods under human forms, but represented them either by symbolic pillars, or by images not of the human type. In his poem, "The Scholar Gipsy," Matthew Arnold imagines how the early Hellene appeared to the Phoenician, whose haunts in the eastern Mediterranean he was beginning to invade : —

> As some grave Tyrian trader, from the sea,
>   Descried at sunrise an emerging prow
> Lifting the cool-haired creepers stealthily,
>   The fringes of a southward-facing brow
>   Among the Aegean isles;
>
> And saw the merry Grecian coaster come,
>   Freighted with amber grapes and Chian wine,
>   Green, bursting figs, and tunnies steep'd in brine,
> And knew the intruders on his ancient home,
>
> The young light-hearted masters of the waves —
>   And snatch'd his rudder, and shook out more sail,
>   And day and night held on indignantly
> O'er the blue Midland waters with the gale,
>   Betwixt the Syrtes and soft Sicily,
>   To where the Atlantic raves
>
> Outside the western straits, and unbent sails
>   There, where down cloudy cliffs, through sheets of foam,
>   Shy traffickers, the dark Iberians come ;
> And on the beach undid his corded bales.

The period at which the Hellenes began gradually to oust the Phoenicians from their trading-stations in the southern Aegean is placed by some as early as the twelfth century B. C., and can hardly have been later than the eleventh. Homer knows Phoenicians in the Aegean only as occasional visitors, the cunning vendors of Oriental wares. The Phoenician left the Aegean to the Hellene, and passed on to found more permanent

seats of industry and trade in the western Mediterranean.

But who are these new comers, the Hellenes,
and with what qualities do they stand forth against
the background of that ancient world at which we
have been glancing?

The history of the Hellenes begins, for us, with
a series of great migrations. When
these movements took place, the country
afterwards known as Greece was occupied by a number of Indo-European tribes, akin
to each other, but, for the most part, unconscious
of the kinship. Such were the Selloi at Dodona
and the Graioi on the Oropus. To these tribes
the only collective appellation which we can give
is that of Hellenes, a modified form of the name
borne by the Selloi. These Hellenes, offshoots
of the Indo-European stem, had forgotten their
own origin, and believed themselves children of
the soil on which they lived. For us, indeed,
they are such. Collectively, these prehistoric
Hellenes represent a civilization which later immigrants found existing in Greece, and partly
destroyed, partly assimilated. These later immigrants consisted, in the main, of tribes akin to
the Hellenes themselves, though neither they nor
the Hellenes knew it. The two earlier streams of
immigration entered the Balkan peninsula from
east and west respectively. From the east came
those who passed through Thrace into the highlands on the further side of the Strymon, and

The first
appearance of
the Hellenes.

were afterwards known as Macedonians. The Thracian tribes whom they displaced were, like themselves, Aryan, but not in any nearer sense akin to the Hellenes. From the west, moving southward, came other immigrants, who occupied Epeirus, Acarnania, and Aetolia. They displaced the Hellenes there, — of whom the Selloi at Dodona were an isolated survival; and they partly obliterated that old Hellenic civilization which can be dimly traced in the heroic legends of Aetolia. A branch of this northwestern immigration passed over into western Peloponnesus, where the settlers in the upper valley of the Peneus came to be known as Eleans, or " Dalesmen."

A third movement took its rise in the centre of the Balkan peninsula, from the forests and upland valleys of northern Pindus. Thence came the primitive " Boeotians," "Thessalians," and "Dorians." The Boeotians issued forth into the land afterwards called Thessaly, and thence, under the pressure of their kinsmen, into Boeotia. Both in Thessaly and in Boeotia the immigrants found an old Hellenic civilization. But the Thessalian aristocracy never acquired more than a tinge of it. The Boeotians assimilated it more largely, though not completely. When the Dorians first appear in history, they have already advanced southwards as far as the highlands north of Parnassus, and possess the sanctuary of the old Hellenic god Apollo at Delphi.

Meanwhile the primitive Hellenes, displaced by these manifold forces, had sought other homes. Some had settled in the islands of the Aegean, or on the coasts of Asia Minor. There they came into collision with other tribes of Indo-European descent, which appear under the collective name of Carians, and were for the most part conquered or absorbed. Other Hellenes passed into Peloponnesus. Under these new conditions, the old divisions of the Hellenes into small tribes were lost, and were replaced by larger aggregates, which may be considered as small nations within the Hellenic nationality, the Aeolian and the Ionian.

It does not fall within my scope to enter upon any detailed discussion as to the origin of the Homeric poems. But I am bound to state the outlines of my belief. I hold that the original nucleus of the Iliad was due to a single Achaean poet, living in Thessaly before the immigration which partly displaced the primitive Hellenes there. This primary Iliad may have been as old as the eleventh century B. C. It was afterwards brought by Achaean emigrants to Ionia, and there enlarged by successive Ionian poets. The original nucleus of the Odyssey was also composed, probably, in Greece proper, before the Dorian conquest of the Peloponnesus; was carried to Ionia by emigrants whom the conquerors drove out; and was there expanded into an epic which blends the local traits of its origin with the spirit of Ionian adventure and Ionian society.

The Iliad is, for us, the first articulate utterance of the Hellenic race, and the oldest picture of Hellenic life. Remembering the salient characteristics of ancient Egypt, Babylonia, Assyria, Phoenicia, let us inquire what are the new tendencies or qualities which the Iliad reveals in this new race.

The Hellenic mind as disclosed in the Iliad.

In the first place, — how foreign to all the sacerdotal traditions of the East is the Hellenic manner of dealing with religion! The Hellenic gods and goddesses are glorified men and women, human in love, hate, and guile, superhuman in power and in beauty ; they speak the same language as the human heroes, — noble, yet simple and direct ; the poet fearlessly relates, for all to hear who will listen, what these deities say to each other as they feast, or debate, or quarrel, in their Olympian home ; when the gods are angry, they are propitiated in the open light of day by all the folk, with dance and song and sacrifice ; there is no dark symbolism, no occult ritual ; there are no animal forms, no hybrid monsters, representative of dread agencies hostile to man ; the hundred-headed Typhon has been vanquished by Zeus, and is a prisoner beneath the earth ; Cerberus is merely the watchdog of Hades. Nor is any prominence given to priests as overseers and interpreters of religion. Priests, in the plural number, are mentioned only twice in the Iliad (9. 575, 24. 221), and both times with reference to local or special rites. We also hear

Religion.

of Apollo's priest at Chryse in the Troad (Il. 1. 37), and at Ismarus in Thrace (Od. 9. 198), but he is merely the guardian of the local shrine. Religion has now its central seat, not in the authoritative lore of a priesthood, not in a close corporation which jealously guards its secrets, but in the free consciousness of the people, who turn for enlightenment only occasionally, at moments of doubt or difficulty, to the soothsayer, the expert in omens. At public sacrifices, the king, as head of the state, takes the foremost part, just as the head of the family does in private worship. The hieratic spirit has given place to the lay spirit. The layman, working as an artist, has asserted the right of the plastic mind over the conception of the deity ; has invested it with the highest beauty that he could imagine; and has made that series of divine types the perpetual possession of his race. To the priesthood of Egypt, or of Babylonia and Assyria, such a treatment of religion would have seemed an audacious impiety, which robbed sacred lore of its mystery, and thereby of its strongest hold upon the hopes or fears of mankind. Nevertheless, no lay disciple of those priesthoods can have felt a truer reverence for the divine than is manifested by the Greek warrior of the Iliad and the Greek wanderer of the Odyssey.

Not less striking is the contrast between the type of monarchy which had prevailed in the East and that which is disclosed by Homer. The

Homeric poems give less prominence to the extent of the royal power than to the provisions for justice and for reasonable liberty by Government. which that power is limited. It belongs to the very essence of Homeric kingship that the king is the divinely appointed guardian of those dooms or precedents, *themistes*, on which the rights of his subjects are founded. To give crooked judgments is the mark of a bad king, who will not escape the vengeance of the gods. The king lays business before his council of elders; the public assembly includes all the freemen of the realm. The Asiatic type of monarchy was, like the Hellenic, constitutional. But Aristotle expresses the difference in Greek terms when he describes the Asiatic monarchy as a constitutional tyranny, tolerated by Asiatics because they were, in his phrase, "more servile by nature;" while he conceives the Greek monarchy as originally a reward conferred upon some signal benefactor of the people, and then continued to the benefactor's descendants. The Greek monarchy of the heroic age is far indeed from that conception of the State which the Greek mind afterwards developed; yet it carries within it the seeds of such a State; the promise of political growth is there, and the spirit of Western civilization.

Thus the Hellenes stand forth, at this early moment, as already exempt from both the forms of despotism which had benumbed or paralyzed human progress in the East. They wear the yoke neither of priests nor of kings.

But, remarkable as this phenomenon is, it does not go far towards illustrating those qualities which made the Hellenes a unique race. The Phoenicians also seem to have reconciled both monarchy and sacerdotalism with a full development of their peculiar energies in new fields of enterprise. The true distinction of the Hellenes is not the mere fact of their escape from deadening agencies ; it is the character, intellectual and moral, to which they owed it. What, then, is this character, as expressed in the first utterance of the race, the Homeric poetry ? We remember the general views of humanity which are exhibited in the sculptures of Egypt and of Assyria. Everywhere we see the king, or some great priest or official, or troops of soldiers, or prisoners, or servants. Man, as seen in those sculptures, either has become superhuman, an image of deified majesty, a sacred and conventional embodiment of imperturbable, pitiless, irresistible power ; or he stands in the presence of his terrible gods, the punctilious and awe-struck ministrant of some exact ritual by which he may hope to propitiate them ; or he is a nameless figure in a multitude who exist only to do the will of their master, to live and toil for him, or to die. Sublimity there sometimes is in these pictures, and sometimes pathos ; but a rigid prescription governs every portraiture ; humanity is depicted only in certain official and conventional aspects ; and the shadow of the despot or the priest rests upon them all.

Now leave the monuments of the Egyptian
temple or the Assyrian palace, and turn
to the pages of the Iliad and the **Odys-** Attitude towards nature
and life.
sey. At once we are in the open air,
and in the sunshine of a natural life. The human
faculties have free play in word and deed. All
the movement, all the beauty and the joy of the
outward world are observed with a spontaneous
freshness of interest and delight. No trammels
of rigid tradition check the utterance of human
feeling, or silence the thoughts awakened by the
known or unknown conditions of mortal destiny.
Achilles, with his brilliant prowess, his chivalry,
his fervor of wrath and of affection, his fine
sensibility to the soothing or strengthening counsels of the gods, and his presage, even when his
glory is in the zenith, of a premature death ;
Andromache, parting from Hector when he goes
forth to battle, and vainly awaiting his return ;
Nausicaa playing at ball with her maidens,
and guiding Odysseus towards the city of her
father ; Odysseus and Penelope, — these are creations that have held the world ever since with
a charm which, so far as we know, they first
revealed, — the charm of truth to nature, united
with an artistic sense of what is beautiful and
pathetic in human life. The Hellene may not
have been the first of mankind who felt these
things, but he was the first who, feeling them,
was able to express them. "What a piece of
work is a man !" cries Hamlet ; "how noble in

reason ! how infinite in faculty ! in form and moving how express and admirable! in action how
like an angel ! in apprehension how like a god !"
This is very much what the Hellene said, and was
the first to say, in the ancient world ; but, if the
words of Hamlet had been indeed Hellenic, they
would have tempered this exulting admiration
with some reference to the limitations of the
human lot.   In those clear outlines and gracious
forms which Homer gives us, we see already the
Homeric sense of measure ; and we can perceive
how intimately this sense is allied with another
characteristic of the race which is also revealed by

Homer, — its intellectual fearlessness.
Fearless de-sire of know-ledge. From the first, the Greek is resolved to
confront the facts of life ; be they good
or evil, he will not seek refuge from them in will-
ful ignorance, or in mysticism ; he will turn his
eyes away from no horror and no pain ; nor,
again, will he suffer them, thus steadily beheld, to
depress his activity.   The Greek was impelled by
a primary law of his nature to know, and in the
light of knowledge to estimate what he could or
could not do.   He possessed, rather as an instinct
than as a result of experience, the sense of proportion ; and this sense, applied to human life as
a whole, produced that abiding consciousness of

Melancholy. its narrow limit which is the source of
Greek melancholy.   When Odysseus
meets the wraith of Achilles in the shades, and
consoles him because he is still a prince there, the

phantom replies : " Nay, speak not comfortably to me of death, great Odysseus ; I would rather be a serf bound to the soil, the hireling of a man with little land or wealth, than bear sway over all the departed." The true Greek seldom forgot that life is short, and that a mortal must think mortal thoughts.

The language of Homeric poetry is another witness to the mind which shaped it. The Homeric Compare Homeric Greek with its elder language. sister, the literary language of ancient India, and the difference is significant. Sanskrit has been the more faithful guardian of old sounds and old forms. The transparency of its structure gives it an unequaled value for students in relation to the whole family of languages to which it belongs. Greek attracts by a different kind of interest. The thought which it suggests is rather, how wonderfully this language has achieved the purposes inherent in its own particular genius. It is an instrument which responds, with happy elasticity, to every demand of the Greek intellect. The forms which it has retained are light, graceful, flexible. It can express the most delicate shades of meaning with the most elegant simplicity ; and this power is due, not only to its organic structure, but also to the tact with which words, expressing the same general notion, have been discriminated in its rich vocabulary. The Greek language is the earliest work of art created by the spontaneous working of the Greek mind.

If those precious fragments of Greek architecture and sculpture which have survived from later centuries had come down without the credentials of their origin, simply as relics of some otherwise unknown race, it would have been neither rash nor fantastic to affirm that, of all the peoples recorded in history, the only one presumably capable of producing such work in art was the same whose thoughts had moulded and whose spirit had chastened the most perfect among the forms of human speech. As an organ of poetry, Greek is nowhere seen to greater advantage than in the Homeric epics. And there, as vividly as anywhere, the language bears the stamp of the imagination which has shaped it. The Greek saw the object of his thought directly and clearly. His first aim in language was to make the expression fit the thought. When an imagination of this kind, unclouded by any haze of literary reminiscence, and free from conscious striving after effect, soars into the region of the marvelous or the ideal, it still commands the obedience of the language which it has disciplined in the field of natural observation. Consider, for instance, the preternatural elements in the Odyssey. The Oriental art which embodied an abstract conception or a mystic dogma in some hybrid or monstrous animal form was merely making an effort of symbolism. The spectator may comprehend the meaning or accept the doctrine, but he does not believe in the monster. The reader of the

Odyssey, on the other hand, who feels the persons to be real, is not robbed of his illusion when Circe changes the hero's companions into swine; or when the roasting flesh of the sun-god's oxen bellows on the spits; or when Poseidon petrifies the Phaeacian ship. The human verisimilitude of the whole disguises the impossibility of the details; we scarcely feel at the moment that they are impossible. But how has this effect been attained? By an imagination which, through habitual contact with what is living and real, has learned to animate fiction also with the breath of life; and which is served here also by a language so faithfully and finely moulded upon nature that, when it clothes a narrative of the miraculous, the very outlines of the garment disarm suspicion as to the form which they invest.

Or consider a still more remarkable achievement in a yet higher sphere, — the evolution of the Homeric Olympus. There *The Homeric pantheon.* was a prehistoric chaos of local cults, in which a host of tribal gods and goddesses competed for each other's prerogatives, with the result that few of such deities possessed a truly distinctive character. The early mythologies had abounded in savage and repulsive traits, such as the story of Chronos swallowing his children. Out of all this confusion and debasement the artistic mind of the Hellenes, as seen in Homer, has brought forth the clear and living types of Olympian godhead, Zeus, Hera, Apollo, Athena, and the rest; each

holding a definite province in the government of
the world, or a special relation to the energies
of mankind; each, too, a person, of a certain
aspect and with certain qualities. These persons
are constantly mingling among men; fighting
hand to hand with them, — aiding or thwarting
them, — enlightening or deceiving them; yet they
never become less than divine, as the Homeric
man never becomes more than human.

The art of sculpture, as applied by Egyptians
and Asiatics to divine beings, was still
in the rigid bondage of priestly tradition, when these Homeric gods, the earliest masterpieces of a free plastic genius, were
delineated by the Greek imagination. The Homeric poetry was, indeed, instinct with the promise of Hellenic art. Such qualities of poetical
thought, such forms of language, announced a
race from which great artists might be expected
to spring. It is true that these Hellenes, whose
intellectual growth was already so remarkable,
and who had already outstripped other nations in
the progress towards a rational life, were still the
pupils of the older civilizations in matters of technical skill. The choice ornaments which the Homeric Greek prizes — the finely wrought silver
bowls, the silver work-baskets on wheels, the em-
broidered robes, the necklaces of amber and gold
— come to Greeks from Phoenicia or Egypt. If
Helbig be right, the general effect of the Homeric
house and of Homeric art was rather Oriental

[marginal note: Homeric poetry as a presage of Greek achievement.]

than properly Hellenic. A visitor to the palace
of Menelaus might have fancied himself at Nine-
veh in the palace of Sanherib, or at Tyre in the
palace of Hiram. The shield of Achilles described
in the Iliad is certainly, as a whole, the creation of the poet's fancy, indebted for details
to Phoenician, Egyptian, and perhaps Assyrian
sources. Yet it illustrates the Hellene's feeling
for such workmanship. And a surer presage of
Greek art is afforded by the sense which we see
in Homer of human beauty, not merely in the
youthful, but in the aged, — as when Achilles
admires the comeliness of Priam, — or even in the
dead, as when the Greeks gather round the corpse
of Hector. Nor is this the only field in which
Homer is unconsciously prophetic of Greek
achievement. If the love of beauty is there, so
also is the love of knowledge and the love of freedom. In those clear and noble tones which rang
out from primitive Ionia with a music never heard
before on earth, there was no uncertain promise
that in generations to come this people would
show the way to mankind in the fearless search
for truth ; that they would strive towards a conception of society which should reconcile individual rights with the public good ; that, wherever a
city of theirs arose, be the surroundings what they
might, it would be a witness to reason, and a foe
to the enslavement of the human mind ; and that,
even when they failed, their influence would still
make always for the cause of light, and never for

the cause of darkness.   No other race has had its
essential qualities so comprehensively interpreted
by its best poetry.   How little would the poetical
literature of the Romans — even if the poems of
Ennius and Lucilius had survived — have sufficed
to acquaint us with the gifts of that imperial people whose true genius is read in the monuments
of their law, or in those massive works which
record their presence throughout the furthest
lands to which the Roman eagles were borne!
Vergil has set forth the mission of Rome in majestic verse; but how pale is the image which it calls
up, compared with that which rises before the
traveler from Nismes to Avignon, when a turn
of the road reveals the stately aqueduct which
Agrippa, the son-in-law of Augustus, threw across
the valley of the Gard, or, when on one of the
old Roman roads in Britain, we stand in the foot-
steps of the legions which once held that distant
outpost of the Empire!   The poetry written in the
English tongue is among the chief glories of the
English-speaking world; but it is the flower of
their spirit, not the index of their capacity.   Of
the Greeks, however, it might be truly said that
their best poetry, rightly understood, is an index
of their capacity, — a special form of their energy
in which the other forms are implicit.   This was
possible, not simply because their genius was
more distinctively intellectual than practical, but
because those qualities of intellect which made
them excellent in poetry were ultimately the same

which made them fruitful in other forms of literature, in science, in art, and in political development. The part assigned to them in the drama
of the nations was to create forms of beauty, to
unfold ideas which should remain operative when
the short bloom of their own existence was over,
and thus to give a new impulse, a new direction, to the whole current of human life. The
prediction which Thucydides puts into the mouth
of the Athenian orator has been fulfilled, though
not in the sense literally conveyed : " Assuredly
we shall not be without witnesses," says Pericles ;
"there are mighty documents of our power, which
shall make us the wonder of this age, and of ages
to come." He was thinking of those wide-spread
settlements which attested the empire of Athens.
But the immortal witnesses of his race are of
another kind. Like the victims of the war, whose
epitaph he was pronouncing, the Hellenes have
their memorial in all lands, graven, not on stone,
but in the hearts of mankind.

I have been endeavoring to show how new a
force the Greek mind was when it first Distinction
appeared in the world. The comparison of the Greeks
among Indo-
has necessarily been with the types of Europeans.
civilization then dominant, — the Egyptian, the
Babylonian and Assyrian, the Phoenician ; and
these were products of races which did not belong
to the Indo-European family. But the separate-
ness of the Greek genius is not less remarkable if
it be compared with that of other Indo-European

races. One illustration may suffice. The great
Sanskrit epics, the Māhābharata and the
Rāmāyana, dating from a much later time than
the Homeric poems, are not only composed in a
language with which Greek, its younger sister,
has so many affinities, but they exhibit, in some
respects, a general analogy to the Iliad and the
Odyssey. Both the Sanskrit epics are of manifold interest, and abound in beauties; they have,
in particular, one charm for the modern mind
with which Homer cannot compete: they are
more romantic. But they are also disfigured by
those faults which spring from a defective sense
of fitness and of measure; they occasionally lapse
into grotesque conceits, or run into exaggeration;
they are the works of poets who were not sure
artists; and, considered as works of art, they must
be placed in a rank altogether below that of the
Homeric poems. And as in India, so elsewhere.
Both the compass and the harmony of those gifts
which were united in the Greek race distinguish
it from every other member of the Indo-European
family. We are reminded of this in the history
of modern art, when some peculiar felicity of invention or of achievement has to be explained by
the fact that different strains of blood have been
blended, and that consequently several branches
of the Indo-European family have contributed to
a result which no one of them could have produced alone. For example, perhaps the most
signal achievement of France in art has been the

creation of Gothic architecture ; and it is pointed
out that the region which was the cradle of that
architecture, the "Royal Domain" of central
France, is one in which the Celtic blood of the
Cymri was blended with the Latin element derived from the Romans, and with the Teutonic
element furnished by the Franks. Here, it is
said, is the complex source of that Gothic style
which blends liberty with self-restraint, audacity
with prudence, science with emotion. Or, again,
our notice is drawn to some sharp limitation of
the artistic faculty in a race with great gifts for
art ; as the Italians, for instance, who reached
such exquisite skill in Renaissance ornament,
failed in the treatment of Gothic detail. Are we
not warranted by what we know of Greek work,
imperfect though our knowledge is, in saying
that no people has yet appeared in the world
whose faculty for art, in the largest sense of the
term, has been so comprehensive ? And there is
a further point that may be noted. It has been
said that the man of genius sometimes is such in
virtue of combining the temperament distinctive
of his nation with some gift of his own which is
foreign to that temperament ; as in Shakespeare
the basis is English, and the individual gift a
flexibility of spirit which is not normally English.
But we cannot apply this remark to the greatest
of ancient Greek writers. They present certainly
a wide range of individual differences. Yet so
distinctive and so potent is the Hellenic nature

that, if any two of such writers be compared, however wide the individual differences may be, — as between Aristophanes and Plato, or Pindar and Demosthenes, — such individual differences are less significant than those common characteristics of the Hellenic mind which separate both the men compared from all who are not Hellenes.   If it were possible to trace the process by which the Hellenic race was originally separated from their Aryan kinsfolk, the physiological basis of their qualities might perhaps be traced in the mingling of different tribal ingredients. As it is, there is no clue to these secrets of nature's alchemy : the Hellenes appear in the dawn of their history with that unique temperament already distinct : we can point only to one cause, and that a subordinate cause, which must have aided its devel-

Influence of land and climate on Greek development.

opment, namely, the geographical position of Greece. No people of the ancient world were so fortunately placed. Nowhere are the aspects of external nature more beautiful, more varied, more stimulating to the energies of body and mind. A climate which, within three parallels of latitude, nourishes the beeches of Pindus and the palms of the Cyclades ; mountain-barriers which at once created a framework for the growth of local federations, and encouraged a sturdy spirit of freedom ; coasts abounding in natural harbors ; a sea dotted with islands, and notable for the regularity of its wind-currents ; ready access alike to Asia and to the western Mediterranean, — these were circumstances happily congenial to the inborn faculties of the Greek race, and admirably fitted to expand them.

Such was the favored land which saw the beginnings of Western civilization. To show how the development of Greek poetry kept pace with Greek life will be the aim of the succeeding lectures in this course.

II

EPIC poetry was the earliest, of a finished form, which the Greeks created; and it had **The Greek definition of Epic.** existed for a long period before any other species was developed. No example of lyric poetry (using that term to include elegiac and iambic) is on record, which can be referred to an earlier date than about 700 B. C. The name "epic" itself, as the Greeks of the classical age understood it, was defined only by its differences from lyric and dramatic. As distinguished from lyric, it meant poetry which was recited, not sung to music; as distinguished from dramatic, poetry which merely narrated. The oldest epics were composed in the hexameter measure; but the term "epic" implied nothing as to metre. The oldest and greatest examples of such poetry dealt with legends concerning heroes; though this again is not contained in the definition. Hence these two traits came to be generally associated with the term "epic." It was understood to mean a poem which narrated heroic action in hexameter verse. But, even in the earliest age of Greece, poems were composed in the epic form which were not on heroic themes. Thus Hesiod's Works and Days, and his Theogony, must be classed as epic; though the former poem has nothing to do with the heroes, and the latter is concerned only with their genealogy. Hesiod and his school used the epic form because it was the only one available for their purpose; and they applied it to any theme which they desired to treat. Hence, for moderns who seek to trace the growth of Greek poetry, and to see how it gave utterance to successive phases of the Greek mind, this term "epic" is inconveniently large; it requires to be defined by a further distinction. The Greeks were content to discriminate their great classes of poetry by external form alone, because the form was regarded as a law (θεσμός) implying certain rules of style and treatment, whatever the subject might be. Hesiod, in the epic form, observes these precepts, after his own fashion, though that fashion is not Homeric: and the Greeks, their artistic sense being so far satisfied, did not feel that it was confusing to class Homer and Hesiod together as epic poets. This was made still easier for them by their way of looking at all poets as teachers: Hesiod is directly a teacher; and they regarded Homer as a teacher also.

The relation of Homer to the development of Greek poetry is, however, totally different from that of Hesiod; and this is the point on which we must fix our attention here. *The highest form of Greek epos is the Homeric.* The highest excellence of Greek epos, as Homer reveals it, is inseparable from the

nature of the Homeric subject-matter; it was
necessary to this highest excellence that the
theme should have an ideal greatness, and that it
should be an organic whole. Only then was it
possible for the Greek mind to show the best
that it could do in this kind. Homeric epos
marks one of the summits of Greek achievement.
When we think of the Greek epic as a chapter
in the evolution of Greek poetry, we must think
of it as represented by the Iliad and the Odyssey.

Further: objection is sometimes made to the
view of the Greek epic period as pre-
ceding the lyric and as clearly marked
off from it, on the ground that, long after
lyric poetry had come into existence, epic poetry
continued to be written. Here, again, we must
distinguish. It is true that between 700 and 400
B. C. we meet with the names of several epic poets,
whose works are now represented only by meagre
fragments; such as Asius, Peisander, Panyassis,
Antimachus, Choerilus. But these, without ex·
ception, are representatives of what, in contradistinction to the Homeric and genuine Hesiodic
work, must be called literary epos. These men
did not continue the natural life of Greek epos;
they were imitators of the great models left by an
earlier age. Then comes the Alexandrian period,
with its artificial heroic epos, such as that of
Apollonius Rhodius; or its didactic epos, like
that of Aratus and Nicander: after which the

Relation of the epic period to the lyric.

annals of Greek epos have nothing better to show than Oppian, Quintus Smyrnaeus, and Nonnus. As to the old Cyclic poems, the more considerable among them did not overlap the lyric period, but came before it.

Clearly, then, the known facts warrant the view that the Greek epic period should be regarded as having closed before the lyric opened. The true epic poetry of Greece had finished its course before the earliest lyric strains were heard. The epos which came later had the form without the soul; it was not characteristic of the Greek genius in this kind.

In striving to imagine the early days of Greek epic poetry we naturally turn to those scenes of the Odyssey where the ancient Greek poet introduces the ancient Greek minstrel. Such passages are at least far nearer in time and spirit than anything else now extant to the days when minstrels sang in the halls of Achaean chiefs; and they are full of suggestion. The suitors of Penelope, holding their insolent revels in the house of the absent Odysseus, compel the minstrel Phemius to sing to them after their feasting. A servant places a lyre in the minstrel's hands; and the lay which Phemius selects to sing concerns the return of the Achaeans from the war at Troy, when Athena vexed them with sore troubles on their homeward voyage. The revelers sit listening in silence. Meanwhile Penelope, who is in an upper room of the house, hears the strain; she

The Greek minstrel. — Scenes in the Odyssey.

descends the stairs, with two of her handmaids, and standing near the entrance of the hall, with her veil drawn over her face, speaks amidst her tears to the minstrel. "Thou knowest many other charms for mortals, deeds of gods and men," she says; "I pray thee, change this piteous strain, which consumes my heart within me." Her son Telemachus gently reproves her. "Why dost thou grudge that the sweet minstrel should gladden us as his spirit moves him? When minstrels sing of woeful themes, it is not their fault; it is the fault of Zeus, who sends the woes. This minstrel is not blameworthy for singing of the evil doom of the Danaoi; he has chosen the newest theme, which will please most." So Penelope goes back silently to her chamber, and weeps for Odysseus, till Athena sends sleep upon her eyelids.

The other scene takes place in the palace of Alcinous, the king of Phaeacia. Odysseus has been shipwrecked, and is now the guest of the king, who does not know who he is. The hall is thronged with Phaeacians, old and young; there has been a sacrifice, and now there is to be a feast. The "herald," or chamberlain, of the king leads in the blind minstrel Demodocus, places him in the midst of the guests, on a high chair inlaid with silver; suspends the lyre on a pin, fixed in a pillar behind the chair; and guides the blind man's hands so that he shall know where to find it; then places a table beside him, with a basket of bread, and a goblet of wine. The feast being

over, Demodocus is stirred by the Muse to sing
the deeds of famous men (κλέα ἀνδρῶν) ; and his
theme is a quarrel between Odysseus and Achilles, — a lay "of which the fame had reached the
wide heaven." Odysseus, sitting unknown among
the guests, draws his purple cloak over his face to
hide his emotion. When the minstrel paused in
his song, and the other guests were applauding or
talking, Odysseus would stealthily wipe away his
tears ; but his royal host perceived it, and presently proposed that the company should go out
to see athletic games. So the chamberlain hangs
up the lyre again, and guides the minstrel out of
the hall. Once again Alcinous makes a banquet
for his guest, and again Demodocus is summoned.
Odysseus sends the minstrel a mess of boar's
flesh as a special honor, and, with praise of his
former singing, asks him to give them a particular lay about the making of the wooden horse, in
which the Greek heroes were hidden, and by
means of which they took Troy. The minstrel
obeys ; and again Odysseus is strongly moved by
the strain. In this instance, we note an interesting phrase : it is said that the minstrel, on hearing
the request of Odysseus, "took up the tale from
that point," — that point, namely, in some longer
lay concerning Troy.

Nor is it only in these memorable passages that
the Odyssey refers to the art of the minstrel.
The swineherd Eumaeus, eager to make Penelope
understand the charm of the newly arrived stran-

ger (Odysseus), has recourse to a simile: " Even
as when a man gazes on a minstrel, whom the
gods have taught to sing words of yearning joy to
mortals, and they have a ceaseless desire to hear
him, so long as he will sing, — even so he charmed
me, sitting by me in the halls."

Thus the minstrel appears in the Odyssey as a
singer whom men believe to be directly moved
by the gods or by the Muse; he sings in the halls
of chieftains, accompanying his song with the
lyre; and his song is ordinarily a lay of moderate
compass, dealing with some episode complete in
itself, such as the making of the wooden horse,
taken from a larger story, such as the tale of
Troy.   But there are two points above all others
that deserve notice.   The first is the
rapt attention with which the audience
listens, — the strong power of the minstrel over their emotions.   This entirely agrees
with the vivid picture of the effects produced, in a
later age (*circ.* 400–350 B. C.), by the Homeric rhapsode, as described in Plato's
Ion.   The other point is the phrase used to de-
note the general class of themes handled by the
minstrels, — the deeds of heroes, κλέα ἀνδρῶν.   It
is the same used in the Iliad to describe the
subjects which Achilles sang to the lyre, for his
own pleasure and that of Patroclus, in his hut at
Troy.

In this phrase itself, however, there is nothing
distinctive.   The early age of almost every people

The Greek
minstrel's
power.

His themes.

can show forms of folk-lore and folk-song which
could be described as the deeds of famous men,
the legendary heroes of the race. The question
is, What was distinctive in the Greek conception
here, separating it from the conceptions formed
by other races ?

The early legends of a people commonly blend
mythology with reminiscences more or less historical ; but the proportions which the two elements bear to each other vary indefinitely in different cases. Sometimes mythology is paramount ;
the national saga serves mainly to preserve weird
images of the supernatural, fantastic creations of
a primitive fancy, which have fascinated the childhood of the race, and have continued to haunt its
mind. As an instance, one might take the earlier
shape of the story on which the German The Nibelun-
Nibelungenlied was founded, — a story genlied.
once common to the whole Teutonic stock. In
the Nibelungenlied itself, no doubt, the mytho-
logical element has dwindled before the ethical,
and history, though in a fantastic disguise, has
contributed the persons of Attila and Theodoric.
But the older Norse version of the story still moves
in a world where dæmonic and magical agencies
reign supreme ; Brunhild is a valkyria, and Si-
gurd can metamorphose himself ; the nominally
human persons scarcely pertain to real humanity.
Or such early folk-song may be directly Early English
based on definite historical events, and war-poems.
adhere pretty closely to facts ; thus the early

war-poems of England in the tenth century, such as the "Battle Song of Brunanbuhr" and the "Song of the Fight at Maldon," concern the real struggles against the Danes. And between these two poles there is an intermediate region, a class of legends in which the basis is historical, but in which a free fancy has given a new complexion to the facts, altering, shifting, combining them, mingling them with alloy, old or new, at its pleasure. This is what has happened, French romances of chivalry: for example, in some of the early French romances of chivalry, the so-called "Chansons de Geste." The great German Karl has become the French Charlemagne, with his capital at Paris instead of Aachen; he goes on crusades, and leads his armies against Jerusalem or Constantinople. But, amidst all these fantasies and impossibilities, the romances preserve the fundamental fact that there was a time when a single emperor ruled over western Europe from the Eider to the Ebro. And the same thing holds good of minor persons; thus the Roland of the romance is killed fighting against Saracens in the Pyrenees; and there was a real knight named Roland, who was indeed killed in Pyrenaean warfare, though his foes were the Gascons. Now the Iliad and the Odyssey are evidently more nearly analogous to the French ro- compared with the Homeric epics. mances of chivalry than to the primitive form of the Nibelungen lay, or to the early war-poetry of England. What exact

measure of historical fact the Iliad contains,
we cannot say: the analogy of the Carolingian
romance would suggest that some Achaean king
may once have held a dominion as extensive as
that of Agamemnon, and that there were struggles in the Troad of the kind which the Iliad
describes ; inferences which are probable on
grounds independent of such analogy. On the
other hand, the supernatural agency is an organic
part of the Iliad ; the Homeric Achilles slays
Hector with the aid of Athena ; we are not logi-
cally justified in eliminating Athena, and still
affirming as a fact that a Greek hero named
Achilles slew a Trojan hero named Hector.

The essential difference between the French romances, considered as legends typical of a class,
and the Homeric epics is this. In the French
romances, widely as they depart from historical
truth, the main interest is afforded by imagination
playing around history. The series of exploits
constitutes the principal charm. These achievements, which the French poets and hearers ascribed to ancestors of their own, form the pith of
the romances ; the characters of the great men
who do them, as, for instance, that of the poetical Charlemagne, however interesting, are of subordinate interest. Now, in the Homeric epics,
the deeds of prowess ascribed to the legendary
ancestors of noble Greek houses or clans were
indeed sources of deep interest and pride to their
descendants ; so, too, were the achievements of

the Greek army, as a whole, against the Trojans.
But the inmost secret of the spell exerted by
Homeric epos does not reside in such sentiments. The supreme and distinctive work of the
Homeric poet was to body forth those
human types in which the Hellenic race
recognized its own ideals, and in con-
templating which it became conscious of itself.
Not the successes won by Achilles, but Achilles
himself, — not the adventures of Odysseus, but
Odysseus himself, — made the Iliad and the Odyssey all that they were to the Greeks. The same
remark applies to the minor human types in each
epic, and, in the Olympian sphere, to the divine
types ; but it is in the central person of either
poem that it is most significant.

The human types in Homeric poetry.

Achilles is a young warrior of transcendent
physical beauty and unequaled prowess ;
he is further characterized by the most
vehement emotions, curbed with difficulty by
strong self-command ; he is a masterly orator, in
whose speaking the most fiery passion is combined
with the keenest power of sarcasm and the utmost
force of argument ; he is also in sympathy with
the gentler graces of human life ; the delight of
his leisure in the camp is to sing the glories of
heroes to the lyre ; his tact and his courtesy are
preëminent ; he is chivalrous and tender towards
the afflicted and the helpless. And he has also a
peculiar pathos. Two fates, as his divine mother
told him, were open to his choice ; he might

Achilles.

remain in Greece, and live to old age, but at the
cost of missing renown ; or he might come to
the war at Troy and win renown, but at the cost
of dying young.   And before the Iliad opens, his
choice has been made.   The presage of an early
doom hovers above him, flitting now and again
like a cloud across the brilliant morning of his
life ; he knows it, and he does not complain.
Modern readers, even students of the classics,
have too often taken their idea of the Homeric
Achilles from the misleading summary of his
character by Horace : " Let him deny that laws
were made for him, and acknowledge no umpire
but the sword."   The very key-note in the character of the Homeric Achilles is his burning indignation at a wrong, at a gross breach of justice ;
he does not represent the sword as against right,
but right as against tyranny.   This is perfectly
marked at the beginning of the Iliad, when
Achilles first appears.   Apollo is plaguing the
Greeks because his priest has been wronged by
Agamemnon.   When the pestilence has been raging for nine days, it is Achilles who summons the
Greeks to the assembly.   He then addresses Agamemnon, and proposes that they shall ask some
soothsayer *why* Apollo is wroth.   On this hint,
without waiting for Agamemnon's invitation, the
seer Calchas at once rises, and says that he can
reveal the cause, if Achilles will promise to protect him from the anger of a great chief ; he does
not say who it is.   Achilles, rising again, bids

Calchas speak fearlessly; no one shall lay a finger on him, — no, not Agamemnon himself. Thus Achilles — who, as yet, has suffered no personal injury, and is acting solely for the common good — stands forth at the outset of the epic as the one chieftain who dares to uphold the public interest, and, in so doing, to brave his suzerain's anger. In the debate which follows, he appears to no less advantage. Calchas declares that Apollo's wrath will not cease until the daughter of Chryses is restored by Agamemnon. The king does not refuse to restore her, but at once demands compensation. Achilles replies that the Greeks have no common stock of property in the camp from which such compensation can be made; the king must wait till Troy has been taken. Agamemnon then makes a most unwarrantable speech; he taxes Achilles with evasion, and declares that, if the Greeks do not provide compensation, he will take it by force. Achilles, thoroughly incensed, and with good cause, denounces him as shamelessly selfish; they are all fighting at Troy in the cause of his family; he himself has the foremost place; yet he actually threatens to despoil his followers. "And now," Achilles ends, "I will go back to Phthia; that is better than to stay here amassing wealth for *thee*." These words are the signal for a torrent of insults from Agamemnon; let Achilles go, — his anger is of no account; nay, the bride of Achilles shall replace the daughter of Chryses, that Achilles may learn to know the power of his chief, and may be a warning to others.

Thus Agamemnon has put himself completely in the wrong: a chivalrous warrior, as Achilles is, might reasonably decline to serve under such a leader, — so violent, so ungrateful, so contemptuous of all reason and fairness, so outrageous in behavior towards comrades who are risking everything for the sake of him and his. It is an essential feature of the Iliad that, though Achilles exceeds measure in the persistence of his resentment, his resentment is, in its origin, perfectly justified. His turbulent emotions are so prominent in the poem that it is all the more needful to observe the restraint which is placed upon them at supreme moments. One such moment occurs after the contumelious speech of Agamemnon just noticed; and there the act of self-restraint is beautifully imaged as obedience to the whisper of a guardian goddess. Achilles is moved to slay Agamemnon on the spot; he is actually drawing his sword from the scabbard, when Athena comes to him from heaven; she glides behind him, and, as he is on the point of darting forward, catches him by his auburn hair; he turns round, and recognizes her; there is an awful divine light in her eyes, but she is invisible to all except himself: she tells him that Hera has sent her, in good will to him and to Agamemnon; he may *rebuke* the king, but he must not draw sword: and then she departs to Olympus. Another such moment is in that noble and touching scene, when Priam comes by night to the Greek camp, to ransom the body

of his son Hector from Achilles. He enters the
young hero's hut unnoticed, and in a moment is
at his feet, clasping his knees and kissing his
hands; and then he makes his prayer to the
young conqueror, asking him to think of his father
Peleus, who may have troubles in his old age, but
is sustained by the hope of seeing Achilles again.
He ends with those famous words, unmatched for
simple and noble pathos: "I have borne such
things as no man on the earth hath ever borne, —
to lift to my lips the hand of the man who hath
slain my son." Achilles raises the old man from
the ground, and places him in a seat, but makes
no sign of granting his prayer; and then Priam
reiterates it. Thereupon Achilles breaks forth:
"Chafe me no more. . . . I myself am minded to
give Hector back to thee. . . . Stir my heart no
more amidst my troubles, lest I keep not my
hands even from thee, though thou art my suppliant, and transgress the commandment of Zeus."
Then he rushes "like a lion" out of the hut, and
gives his orders as to making the corpse of Hector ready for Priam to take home. That dread of
his lest he should slay his aged and helpless guest
is the measure of the bitter and terrible struggle
in his soul. His grief and rage for the death of
his friend are unabated; he feels intensely that,
even now, the ransoming of Hector's corpse may
be a dishonor to the memory of Patroclus. But
he also knows that Zeus commands him to accept
the ransom; and he feels a deep compassion for

Priam. That cry of his, "Chafe me no more,"
marks the extremity of the tension; he can master himself; but he must be let alone to do his
hard duty in the light of his own thoughts.

It is well to remember these aspects of Achilles; to notice that there is more in him than the
brilliancy of the warrior, on whom the panoply
made by Hephaestus flashes "like the gleam of
blazing fire, or of the sun as it arises;" more,
too, than his tempestuous passion, or his splendid
efficiency alike in action and in speech; there is
also that intrepid championship of the public
good, that burning zeal against high-handed op-
pression, that fount of chivalrous compassion, and,
not least, that sense open to the admonitions or
behests of the gods, compelling him to hold his
own fiercest impulses in check, even when they
are straining in the leash, and he mistrusts his
own power to control them. This Homeric Achilles is a type in which the Hellenic age which
gave birth to it saw its own ideal of a glorious
manhood to which the freshness of youth still
remained, — manhood with all its energies of
body and soul in radiant vigor; tinged, also, with
that characteristically Greek melancholy which
springs from a sober recognition of a limit to the
human lot, and sets a boundary to hope, though
without inducing either apathy or complaint.
There is one respect, indeed, in which the Homeric Achilles might seem to contravene an instinct of the Greek nature : is he not deficient in

the sense of measure? When he spurns the en-
voys of Agamemnon, though they offer the am-
plest reparation, and refuses to forego his wrath
until the Greeks shall have been reduced to ex-
tremities, he certainly violates the Greek conception of what is fitting in mortal men. He acts
more like one who is possessed by Atè, — so the
Greeks of the fifth century would have felt, — and
exposes himself to the jealous anger of the gods.
But we must remember that this youthful warrior
belongs to the youth of the race that conceived
him. In him they expressed their ideal of splendid and many-sided force; in him, too, they saw
such an equipoise of faculties as their artistic instinct required in typical manhood: his body has
not been developed at the expense of his mind;
he is a great warrior, but also a great orator; he
can touch the lyre no less than wield the sword.
And in this aspect he expresses the Greek sense
of measure: he is a harmoniously developed human being. On the moral side, that sense of
measure is again represented by his acts of self-
mastery, — as in the scenes with Agamemnon
and Priam. That his feelings are, in themselves,
violent and excessive, results from the effort of
poetry, in a simple and vigorous age, to express
human nature in its highest intensity; Achilles
must be peerless in action; he must be unique
also in vehemence of emotion, — of anger, and of
love.

Odysseus also is an ideal type; but he is not

lifted above ordinary emulation in the same degree as that dazzling embodiment of
youthful force and beauty which is pre- Odysseus.
sented by the son of Peleus. Horace, who
scarcely appreciates the Homeric Achilles, is
more felicitous when he describes Odysseus as an
instructive pattern of what can be done by manliness and wisdom. This hits the point, — that the
Greeks saw in Odysseus no unapproachable hero,
but the great exemplar of certain qualities which
every one might cultivate. Greek poetry, with
its usual tact, does not make Odysseus young.
He is a middle-aged man of the world. His most
prominent trait is the quick-witted versatility
which can deal with every fresh difficulty as it
arises. His intellectual power often gives him,
too, a large measure of foresight. But the Homeric Odysseus, be it observed, is not invariably
prudent. Sometimes, when the most deadly danger is imminent, he fails in common prudence,
through too much curiosity, or through a spirit
too sanguine or too audacious, which leads him to
tempt fate. Take, for instance, his adventure in
the cave of the Cyclops. When he and his comrades reach the cave, Polyphemus is absent. The
comrades propose that they should take the
cheeses, the kids, and the lambs, and make off to
their ship. But no, Odysseus is bent on seeing
Polyphemus, and, oddly enough, professes to
think that the master of the cave may prove hos-
pitable. So there they stay, eating the cheeses of

the Cyclops, till he returns; when Odysseus
speaks, and, with a certain effrontery, expresses a
hope that he and his party, thirteen in number,
may receive entertainment. On being asked
where he has left his ship, he answers with the
ready falsehood that it has been wrecked. The
Cyclops, with an indignation not wholly unwarrantable, replies, not in words, but by cooking
two of the companions for his evening meal; and
all the troubles begin. Not content with having
brought his friends to this pass, Odysseus, when
at last he puts to sea with the six survivors, must
needs shout back a defiance to the giant, who replies by breaking off the top of a mountain, and
throwing it at the ship, which it narrowly misses.
But even this is not enough. When they have
got a little further, Odysseus shows signs of wish-
ing to hail the Cyclops again, and his comrades
implore him to be silent. " Foolhardy that thou
art, why wouldst thou rouse the savage to
wrath ? " " But," says Odysseus in telling the
story, "they prevailed not on my lordly spirit."
And so he shouts again to Polyphemus : " Cyclops, if any shall ask thee who put out thine eye,
say that it was Odysseus, the waster of cities, son
of Laertes, who lives in Ithaca." This leads to
a short dialogue, the end of which is that the Cyclops hurls a huger crag than before, which grazes
their rudder. Another instance of his rashness is
when he forgets one of Circe's express warnings,
as they are nearing Scylla, and stands full armed

at the prow of his ship, attracting her notice by his defiance.

This occasional excess of daring is an important trait in the Homeric Odysseus; it distinguishes him from the cold, cautious, even mean-souled Odysseus of later writers. His true distinction, in the Odyssey, is that he has wit enough to extricate himself from any difficulty, and fortitude enough to bear whatever the gods send. He is sometimes found in situations trying to heroic grandeur, as when the ram conveys him out of the cave, or when he clings "like a bat" to the wild fig-tree above Charybdis; who can imagine Achilles in such positions? But even then he is heroic, with the heroism of supreme ingenuity. And his companions supply the measure of his superiority to commonplace men. The only thing in which they ever have the better of him is commonplace caution, and then it merely serves to bring out his advantage in intellect. He never yields to merely sensuous temptation, and he never defies the known will of the gods, as his companions do when they eat the oxen of the sun-god in Thrinacria. But strong as he is, he is in no way raised above human infirmity. The song of the Sirens woos mortals to the isle where all knowledge shall be theirs, — knowledge of what has been, and of what shall be hereafter upon the earth. The finer the spiritual ear, the more perilous the allurement of that promise; and Odysseus endures a harder ordeal than his grosser comrades, whose labor is needed to row the ship swiftly past that shore, and whose ears are meanwhile sealed with wax against the sounds which, for them, would have had less meaning.   But he, lashed to the mast, must listen to that song ; and his own will would have been too weak, if more than human counsel had not warned him beforehand that he must place himself out of his own power, until those sounds die away over the sea.

That home which he sought through so many wanderings and trials was the true centre of his affections.   The unwilling guest of Calypso in the far west, he yearned for the day when he might see were it but the smoke rising from his own land.   "There is nothing better or nobler," he says to the maiden Nausicaa, "than when man and wife are of one heart and mind in a house." And when at last he reaches Ithaca, and when, still in his disguise, he converses with Penelope, how touching is the anxiety to guard her against too sudden a shock of joy, which appears in his manner of gently preparing her mind for the announcement that her husband has returned. He pretends to be a Cretan, a certain Aethon, who has known Odysseus ; yes, and he has heard on good authority that Odysseus is safe — that he is in Thesprotia — nay, that he will soon be in Ithaca ; and he can say even more, — he can solemnly assure her, as his conviction, that she will soon recover him: " In the same year Odysseus shall come home, as the old moon wanes and the new is born." To the last, he has his moments of despondency. As he lies sleepless in the porch of his own house, on the rude couch allotted to him as a poor and unknown stranger, he muses how he can ever prevail against the suitors, — one man against so many ; he chides his own misgivings ; but he cannot allay them. Then Athena comes to him from heaven, stands above him, and comforts him : " O hard of belief ! Many can trust in a weaker friend than I am, — in a mortal friend ; but I am divine, and I preserve thee to the end." Such is the Homeric Odysseus ; no superhuman paragon, but an able, nimble-witted, brave, patient man, who fights or devises his way through many trials, not without lapses from prudence, not without experience of discouragement, but with a sound brain and a warm heart, and, thanks to the gods, with final success.

Such clear human types as these, instinct with the very essence of the Greek spirit, give to the Homeric epics that living and abiding human interest — first of all for the Greeks themselves, and then for people of every race and age — which distinguishes them from all other poems of war or adventure, how rich soever in the splendor of battle or the charm of wonderland. Here is the indwelling principle of life in the Homeric poetry ; but it is a harder thing to describe the characteristics of the form in which that soul is clothed. If one should say, " Read the Iliad and the Odyssey, or parts

The form of Homeric poetry.

of them, in the original ; that is the only way to
obtain any adequate sense of their distinction in
respect to form," he might seem to be evading his
task ; and yet that is strictly true ; true, not only
as it is, more or less, of all great poetry, but in a
special degree. Translation, even the best, though
it be the work of a poet, will not help far ; still
less will analysis, be it ever so skillful and so subtle. Nevertheless, there is one thing which any
competent guide can do for those who are only
about to read Homer ; he can assist in orientating
their minds ; he can aid them in placing themselves at the right point of view ; if he cannot tell
them what Homer is, he can at least help them to
see what Homer is not. A generation has scarcely
elapsed since it was possible for an accomplished
scholar to include the following epithets among
those which he gave to Homer's style : — "gar-
rulous" and "quaint ; " also to say, " Homer rises
and sinks with his subject, — is prosaic when
it is tame, is low when it is mean." Mr. Matthew Arnold's " Lectures on Translating Homer "
showed once for all how erroneous is the conception which these epithets imply ; we may differ
from him on some points, but nothing could be better than what he says as to the four cardinal qualities of Homer, — plainness of thought, plainness
of style, nobleness, and rapidity. Each

Homeric
plainness of   can best be illustrated by a contrast.
thought.

    First, then, — plainness of thought.
Agamemnon says in Homer : " There will be

a day when sacred Ilios shall perish." How
does the Elizabethan translator, Chapman, render
this ?

" And such a stormy day shall come, in mind and soul I know,
  When sacred Troy shall *shed her tow'rs, for tears of overthrow.*"

The addition of the epithet "stormy" to the
word "day" might pass ; but the thing by which
Chapman violates plainness of thought, and is
therefore un-Homeric, is the idea of comparing
Troy's towers, as they fall, to tears which Troy
sheds at her own ruin. This is not a mere pad-
ding out of the original ; it is a new thought, of
which the original has nothing ; and moreover it
is a fantastic thought, — a conceit. The Elizabethan age was fond of conceits ; it was a puerile
extravagance in the use of the newly recovered
imagination. But if the Greek mind ever went
through such a stage, that stage lies far behind
Homer. When Pope said that Chapman writes,
not like Homer, but as Homer might have written
at an immature age, he was so far quite right.
The proneness to "conceits" is a fault of imma-
turity.

Then as to plainness of style. Sarpedon is
exhorting Glaucus to fight against the _{Plainness}
Greeks: "I would not urge thee," he _{of style.}
says, "if men could live forever. But as it is,
since ten thousand fates of death beset us always,
— forward! Either we shall give glory to a foe-
man, or he to us."

Pope translates : —

> " But since, alas ! ignoble age must come,
> Disease, and death's inexorable doom,
> The life which others pay, let us bestow,
> And give to fame what we to nature owe."

The two last verses are an expansion of the one Greek word, ἴομεν, — " forward ! " — and how the balanced rhetoric destroys its simple force !

Note, in passing, that these two qualities, plainness of thought and plainness of style, are wholly distinct.   A plain thought may be clothed in artificial language, when the result is usually bathos, as in that well-known example, where " open the bottle and cut the bread " becomes, —

> " Set Bacchus from his glassy prison free,
> And strip white Ceres of her nut-brown coat."

Or a plain style may convey a curious thought, as when Lady Macbeth says, —

> " When you durst do it, then you were a man ;
> And to be more than what you were, you would
> Be so much more the man."

Then thirdly, nobleness. Homer's manner is noble, whatever the subject may be, as *Nobleness.* he is always also simple and unconstrained ; and here the snare for the modern translator is that, in trying to be unconstrained, he is apt to become ignoble ; that is, to use some word, recommended by the easy air which it gives, of which the associations are too familiar, or too prosaic — in a word, too low for poetry.

Chapman falls into this snare, when he renders the words spoken by the Homeric Zeus concerning the immortal steeds of Achilles — ἆ δειλώ, "ye hapless ones!" — by a phrase which, though idiomatic, is too colloquial — "poor wretched beasts!"

Lastly, Homer is rapid. In combining this rapidity with unvarying nobleness, the Homeric poems are unique. Homeric ^{Rapidity.} rapidity has two distinct sources. The first and most essential is the quick movement of the poet's mind. His thoughts are direct ; they are ever darting onward ; and he does not retard their progress by details of a merely ornamental kind. "Sing, goddess, the wrath of Achilles," says Homer ; and in his first verse he has announced his theme. Contrast the opening of "Paradise Lost" : —

> "Of man's first disobedience and the fruit
> Of that forbidden tree whose mortal taste
> Brought death into the world and all our woe,
> With loss of Eden, till one greater Man
> Restore us, and regain the blissful seat,
> Sing, Heavenly Muse."

Observe that this first source of Homeric rapidity is not a necessary or universal characteristic of Greek epic poetry as such ; Hesiod does not possess it. It is distinctive of Homeric epos ; and though it belongs to both the Iliad and the Odyssey, it is in the Iliad that we chiefly feel this rushing impetus of mind. The other cause of Homeric rapidity is a joint result of language and metre. Greek has naturally a lighter and swifter movement than, for instance, Latin; and the Greek hexameter, though its rhythm varies so much in different hands, is always lighter and more rapid than the Latin hexameter. The opening lines of the Iliad are, again, a supreme example of this.

The twenty-second book of the Iliad is the climax of the poem. Achilles chases Hector round the walls of Troy, and slays him. Consider the enormous difficulty of treating this simple theme in such a manner that it should be a worthy climax for an epic on the great scale of the Iliad, one so rich in thrilling and varied pictures of warfare; and then observe how the Homeric poet has managed it.

The climax of the Iliad in Book XXII.

At the beginning of the book, Hector is standing outside the Scaean gate, and Achilles is rushing towards him over the plain; Priam and Hecuba on the ramparts implore their son to seek refuge in the city, but he is deaf to their prayers. Then Achilles comes up, and begins chasing Hector round the walls. Here occurs the first problem for the poet. The pursuit must not be too brief; that would rob both the heroes of glory. And, in fact, they make three rounds of the city walls. But how is the poet to maintain, and gradually raise, the excitement of so prolonged a race? How is he to provide that his hearer or reader shall follow that race to the very end, with an interest which not only shall not flag, but shall increase from moment to moment? He has recourse to one of the greatest but most difficult secrets of Homeric epos, — the blending _{Divine and} of divine with human action. Achilles, _{human action.} chasing Hector, has completed two circuits, and the third is in progress; the intense excitement of the pursuit, watched by Trojans from the ramparts and by Greeks from the plain, is marked by these crowning words — "*and all the gods beheld.*" The poet then immediately proceeds: "*And to them* spake the Father of gods and men." In an instant we have been wafted from the plain of Troy to Olympus, and are listening to a debate among the gods, which ends in Athena obtaining leave to help Achilles, and darting down to earth. The third circuit is now drawing to a close, and Apollo inspires Hector with a supreme effort. And the third circuit is all but completed, when Zeus in heaven uplifts the golden scales, and weighs the fates of the two men; the scale which contains the fate of Hector sinks, and he is doomed beyond recall. Athena now makes Achilles halt. Hector, she tells him, shall be persuaded to turn back and face him; she takes the form of Deiphobus, Hector's brother, and emboldens him to confront his foe; in the words of overweening confidence which Hector utters — so unlike his former misgivings — we feel, with a certain horror, that the power of the goddess has not been over his body alone; she has hurt his mind.

And when the phantom of Deiphobus vanishes, Hector himself, sane once more, knows that he must die. His last rush against Achilles has the fury of despair; while the light that flashes from the spear of his foe is likened to the steady ray of Hesperus, fairest of the stars in heaven. He falls, — his dying prayer for funeral rites is spurned, — and he expires after prophesying the doom of his conqueror. Thus the movement of the human action to its goal has been diversified at three moments by divine intervention: the appeal of Athena to her father, the weighing of the fates by Zeus, the deluding of Hector by Athena. And what is peculiarly Homeric in this is that it is managed without impairing the probability of the human action. Achilles and Hector do not seem less real, their deeds do not follow each other less naturally, because Athena interposes. The supernatural agency, on the other hand, is not mechanical, as that of Vergil's Olympus is apt to be. Athena, counseling Achilles, while invisible to Hector; restoring the spear, vainly hurled by Achilles, to his hand, assuming the semblance of Deiphobus, and then suddenly disappearing, — Athena is a being not less real than the mortals; the light of her beautiful and terrible presence seems to flash upon the battle-field, and again to vanish. Homeric poetry alone has been able to create a sphere in which gods and men thus mingle; in which the energies of men are tested to their height by the direct pressure of a superhu-

man force, while the gods become only more lumi-
nously divine by moving upon the earth among
men.

This twenty-second book of the Iliad also
illustrates two other characteristics of
Homeric epos, — the use of direct speech, Homeric use
of direct
and the use of simile. In both of these speech.
Homer has set the example to later poets ; but
here, again, we should note what is distinctively
Homeric.   When Achilles has stricken down Hector, he cries exultingly, " Aye, Hector, when thou
wert despoiling Patroclus, thou thoughtest to be
safe, and didst not reck of me, who was afar.
Thou fool !   But, far from him, at the hollow
ships, I was left behind, mightier to avenge ; and
I have laid thee low.   Thou shalt be foully torn
by dogs and birds, but he shall have honor in his
death from the Achaeans."   These few words reveal the inmost mind of Achilles, — his passionate
grief, his passionate desire to avenge his comrade ; they explain his ruthlessness towards Hector.   This is the more peculiarly Homeric use of
direct speech, — when it serves to bring a motive,
or a situation, into clear relief.   Hence a man's
thoughts are often given as words spoken by him
to his own soul, as Hector's audible thoughts are
when Achilles is drawing near.

Simile, again, in its Homeric use, is never
merely ornamental, but always intro-
Use of simile.
duces a moment, or a thing, which the
poet wishes to render impressive.   He prepares

us for it by first describing something like it, only more familiar. Thus the chase of Hector by Achilles occasions four similes, appropriate to successive moments. Achilles, as he starts in pursuit, is likened to a falcon when it swoops after a dove. As the chase draws towards a close, it is compared to a chariot-race when the chariots round the turning-point of the course and the goal is in sight. As Hector, now almost spent, tries to keep close under the walls, and Achilles again drives him out towards the plain, we have the image of the fawn whom the hound will not suffer to crouch under a bush. And lastly Achilles, when, though gaining on Hector, he cannot overtake him, suggests the admirably vivid simile of a man in a dream, who sees some one flying before him, but seems unable to move in pursuit. Other parts of the Iliad furnish examples of simile, which are in themselves more brilliant and elaborate, — such as that in the eighteenth book, perhaps the most splendid of all the similes, in which the flame flashing from the golden cloud with which Athena has encircled the head of Achilles is likened to the beacon-fire which blazes up at sunset from some beleaguered island, a signal for aid to the neighboring isles and coasts. But nowhere is the Homeric purpose of simile more clearly seen than in the series just mentioned, which so vividly marks the course of the supreme struggle between the two champions.

Thus far we have been considering some of the

principal characteristics which distinguish the Homeric epics from all others. It will be well, next, to notice certain features which belong more especially to the Odyssey. And then, passing from Homeric to Hesiodic epos, we shall find it instructive to observe some of the broad differences between them.

III

In any just perspective of European poetry, the resemblance between the Iliad and the Odyssey must always, of course, be far more striking than the difference. Both present ideal human types, both blend divine and human action, both unite plain thought, plain style, nobleness, and rapidity, in a manner which broadly separates them from all other compositions. To those who regard the epics from a little distance, and not from those closer points of view which have been gained by modern criticism, it will not appear astonishing that this common Homeric character should even have been regarded as showing the work of one mind; for undoubtedly the stamp of mind seen in both epics is one which has no comparable record in any third poem that could be named.

Nevertheless, the differences between the Iliad and the Odyssey, which every reader feels, require to be expressly noted. If we omit to do so, we shall not adequately appreciate the range of power which marked this early age of Greek poetry.

Differences between the Iliad and the Odyssey.

The material of the Iliad is furnished chiefly by warfare or debate. These interests are not wholly absent from the Odyssey, but they hold

a subordinate place, and they have an inferior
degree of animation. When Odysseus slays the
suitors in the banquet-hall, we have, indeed, a full
account of the fight, but not the tone of a fight in
the Iliad; the suitors have no chance against
Odysseus, who is here a personified Nemesis
rather than a mere combatant. The Ithacan assembly in the second book of the Odyssey is
perhaps most in the manner of the Iliad, but it
is not highly effective in itself; since the appeal
of Telemachus is evidently doomed to failure from
the outset, and he has no remedy. The chief
value of the scene consists in exhibiting the insolence of the suitors, and in making us feel that a
retribution, however tardy, must one day overtake
them.

As a whole, the Odyssey derives its charm from
two sources, — narrative of adventure, and description of social life. In respect to both these
elements, it moves in a region which is almost
wholly foreign to the Iliad; and in both it has
qualities peculiar to itself.

The twelfth book may serve to illustrate the
manner in which the Odyssey narrates
adventure. It contains the parting of Style of narrative in the Odyssey.
Odysseus and his comrades from Circe;
the Sirens; Scylla; the impiety of the comrades
in Thrinacria; their destruction; and the narrow escape of Odysseus from Charyb- Brevity and simplicity.
dis. The first thing that we note is
the brevity and simplicity. These marvelous inci-

dents, coming one after another, are told quite plainly, without the least attempt to heighten them by elaboration or comment; there is enough detail to produce an effect of reality, but no more. Thus, after briefly describing Charybdis, the hero says, "We had our eyes bent towards her, in fear of destruction; but meanwhile Scylla snatched six of my companions out of my hollow ship, — the bravest and strongest of them all. As I turned my glance back to the ship, and then in search of my comrades, all at once I espied their hands and feet as they were lifted on high, and they cried aloud to me in their agony, and called me by my name for the last time. Even as a fisherman on a headland, with his long rod, throws his baits to ensnare the little fishes, casting the horn of an ox of the fields into the deep, and when he has hooked his fish, casts it writhing ashore, so writhing were they lifted up to her cave; and there she devoured them, shrieking in her gates, while they stretched forth their hands to me in their dread struggle. That was the most piteous thing ever I saw with mine eyes, in all my toil when I was searching out the paths of the sea."

He says no more on that subject, but continues thus: "Now when we had escaped the rocks, and dread Charybdis and Scylla, then we soon came to the fair island of the god," — Thrinacria.

This episode of Scylla, so naturally and vividly told, fills only sixteen lines. The entire series of

adventures in the twelfth book occupies only 453
lines. A like plainness and absence of prolixity
mark the narratives throughout. We observe the
comparison of Scylla to a fisherman, — introduced,
as it might have been in the Iliad, to mark a
crisis. But, since the Odyssey, owing to the nature of its subject, has fewer moments of concentrated excitement than occur in the battles
of the Iliad, it has fewer similes, — only about
forty, as against the Iliad's 180. The Iliad is an
epic full of dramatic force ; further, it is not only
noble, but preëminently an example of the grand
style, as in the description of Apollo descending
from heaven to smite the Greeks with pestilence :
"The arrows clanged upon the shoulders of the
god in his wrath, as he moved ; and his coming
was in the likeness of night." The Odyssey is
rather the model of how a story should flow ; it
contains examples of the grand style, as when
Circe says to her guests, on their return from
the voyage to the nether world, "Men overbold,
who have gone down alive to the house of Hades,
that ye should twice know death, while other men
die once ;" but its distinctive nobleness is a noble
charm, especially in scenes of peace, and, above
all, of domestic life.

The comparative absence of that dramatic force
which belongs to the Iliad is compen- Picturesque
sated in the Odyssey by a peculiar in- effects.
stinct for picturesque effect. Thus, when Ody-
seus and his son are removing the arms from the

hall to the armory by night, Telemachus suddenly cries: "Father, this is a great marvel that I see with mine eyes; yes, the walls of the hall, and the fair spaces between the pillars, and the beams of pine, and the pillars that run aloft, are bright as it were with flaming fire. Verily some god is within, of those that hold the high heaven."

One other example may be given. When Odysseus is about to enter the palace of the Phaeacian king, Athena throws a cloud around him, to shroud him from the eyes of those who might forbid him to enter. Going onward unseen, he comes at last into the presence of King Alcinous and Queen Arêté. He throws himself in supplication before the queen. At that moment the wondrous mist melts away from him, and silence falls on the Phaeacians, as they marvel at the suppliant. This instinct for the picturesque, into which color and grouping enter, is akin to the dramatic sense, yet distinct from it, and also from the Hellenic sense of clear and beautiful outline. In both the examples just given, one condition is suddenness; the fancy to which such impressions come with a bright surprise is nimble and open, — quick to see the supernatural around it.

Thoroughly congenial to it is that strain of
Magical or
fairy lore.
magical or fairy lore which pervades the Odyssey. This element is not wholly absent from the Iliad; there is the horse Xanthus, speaking with a human voice; there are the self-moving tripods of Hephaestus, and his golden

handmaids who can move, think, and speak. In
the Iliad, however, such things are rare and inci-
dental, whereas they belong to the very texture
of the other epic. The magical herb "moly"
given by Hermes to Odysseus; Ino's magical
veil which saves him from drowning; the por-
tents in Thrinacria, when the flesh of the oxen
bellowed on the spits, and the hides stripped from
them began to move; the Phaeacian ship turned
to stone; the second-sight of the seer Theocly-
menus, — these are instances which occur at once.
Such marvels, it may be remarked, express a side
of the Ionian fancy which had been developed by
maritime adventure, as other aspects of Ionian
character are seen in the sensuous tendencies of
the hero's comrades, or, again, in the graces of
social intercourse which give such a charm to
the epic. Both as a story of voyages and as a
picture of civilization, the Odyssey bears, more
strongly than the Iliad, the stamp of Ionia.

Another trait which pervades the narratives of
the Odyssey, further distinguishing it The divine
from the Iliad, is the mode of conceiv- agency.
ing that divine agency which is blended with the
human. In the Iliad, Olympus is a mountain
from whose heights the gods descend; the peaks
of Ida or of Samothrace are stations from which
the gods observe men; an Olympian debate has
all the reality of a debate on the earth; the
divine action upon men either is physical, or consists in the transmission of commands to them by

a divine messenger who appears in visible shape. In the Odyssey a spiritual element enters more largely into the dealing of the deities with mortals. Thus Odysseus says to his son, "When Athena of deep counsel *shall put it into my heart*, I will give thee a sign;" and faith in the gods has become a more spiritual feeling. Telemachus says that Zeus and Athena are the best of allies, "though their seat is in the clouds on high." And the image of Olympus itself has become more ethereal: it is a far-off place, "where, as men say, is the seat of the gods that standeth fast forever. Not by winds is it shaken, nor ever wet with rain, nor doth the snow come nigh thereto, but the clearest air is spread around it, without a cloud, and a pure light floats over it; therein the blessed gods are glad eternally." A good instance of this difference between the two epics may be found in the twelfth book of the Odyssey. When Odysseus discovers that, while he slept, his companions have slain the oxen of the Sun-god, he cries aloud to father Zeus in his anguish. And then he relates a short scene among the gods: the nymph Lampetie goes swiftly to Helios, the Sun-god, and tells him that his oxen have been slain. Helios then addresses Zeus and the assembled gods, declaring that, unless he is compensated for his oxen, he will shine no more over the earth; he will go down to Hades, and shine among the dead. Zeus, in reply to this threat, promises that he will wreck the

ship of the offenders. The whole scene occupies
only thirteen lines. If it is compared with a parallel incident of the Iliad, — the scene between
Zeus and Athena in the twenty-second book, which,
like this, precedes a catastrophe on earth, — it will
be felt how much less of human-like realism there
is in the passage of the Odyssey. There is a
further difference ; Odysseus feels bound to explain how he came by this knowledge ; and so he
adds that he had heard it from the nymph
Calypso, who herself had heard it from Hermes,
the messenger of the gods. Now in the Iliad
there is no example of such a reply to anticipated
skepticism ; when deeds done, or words spoken,
among the gods are related in the Iliad, the
narrator is the poet himself, who is supposed to
know them by inspiration. The only exception
is Agamemnon's narrative, in the nineteenth book
(95–136), of the discussion in Olympus before the
birth of Heracles, — a passage which seems to
have been interpolated in the Iliad from an epic
Heracleia.

The last distinctive trait of narrative in the
Odyssey which we shall notice is an Traits verging
occasional approach of the tone of com- on comedy.
edy, as moderns would deem it. Thus Odysseus says, after relating how he had warned his
comrades against Charybdis, " I did not go on to
speak of Scylla, lest haply they should give up
rowing, and hide themselves in the hold." This
savors to us of comedy, because it is so opposite

to the heroic; but the poet did not intend it to be comic; the quality in him which it indicates is *naïveté.* So, again, when the men snatched by Scylla are compared to fish wriggling at the end of an angler's line, the comparison is to us grimly grotesque; but the poet's aim was simply to make the horror vivid. And everywhere, even in such touches, the style of the Odyssey preserves its Homeric nobleness.

Let us turn now to that other source, besides narrative of adventure, to which the Odyssey owes Pictures of   its peculiar charm, namely, the descrip social life.   tions of social life. Here the key-note is given by the position of women in the Homeric age; and that position, as exhibited in the Odyssey, is essentially the same of which the Iliad affords glimpses. But the Iliad, an episode of warfare, can give glimpses only; it is reserved for the Odyssey to furnish more complete pictures. The central point is the sanctity of marriage, which is not merely the Homeric rule, but Position of   a rule with few and narrowly limited women.   exceptions. The position of the Homeric wife in her own home may be best stated by saying that it is essentially the same as it is in Christian countries to-day, and totally unlike the position ordinarily held by the Athenian wife in the fifth and fourth centuries B. C. If Odysseus and Penelope were the only wedded couple whose relations were portrayed in the Odyssey, it might be argued that they could not be taken as a nor-

mal instance, since conjugal loyalty is the special
point of their story. But the possible objection
disappears when we consider the other cases, —
Alcinous and Arêtè, Menelaus and Helen: the
position of the wife is similar in all three examples. The hero and heroine of the poem may
then be safely regarded as expressing, though in
a high form, the general feeling of Greeks in the
poet's age. We remember the frank words of
Odysseus to Calypso: " Be not wroth with me
hereat, goddess and queen. Myself I know it
well, how wise Penelope is meaner to look upon
than thou, in comeliness and stature. But she is
mortal, and thou knowest not age or death. Yet
even so, I wish and long day by day to fare homeward and see the day of my returning." Not less
expressive are the words in which Penelope asks
her husband's pardon for not having welcomed
him when he first came in disguise, — she so
dreaded, so she says, to be deceived. In truth,
her slowness to believe is the best measure of her
wish to believe. Of Arêtè, the wife of King
Alcinous, it is said: " She hath, and hath ever
had, all worship heartily from her dear children,
and from her lord Alcinous, and from all the folk,
who look on her as a goddess, and greet her with
reverent speech, when she goes about the town."
When Odysseus is about to present himself in the
palace of Alcinous, Nausicaa, the king's daughter,
gives him this counsel, after describing to him
how he will find the king and queen together in

the great hall : " Pass thou by him, and cast thy
hands about my mother's knees, that thou mayest
see quickly and with joy the day of thy returning,
even though thou art from a very far country. If
but *her* heart be kindly disposed toward thee, then
is there hope that thou shalt see thy friends, and
come to thy well builded house, and thine own
country."

Nausicaa herself is not only the most charming
girl in ancient literature, — so charming, that one
shrinks from making her the subject of prosaic
comment, — but teaches us more than perhaps
any other person as to the position of her sex in
that age. It is at once a proof of the freedom
which she enjoyed, and of the reverence for women which such freedom implies, that her father
should allow her to drive with no escort but that
of her handmaids to a distance from the city. (In
Corfu, where Canóni Bay is the traditional scene
of her meeting with Odysseus, the popular version of the story assumes that she was accompanied by her mother.) But the Homeric description of her meeting with Odysseus is the most instructive passage, and the most beautiful. When
the other maidens are scared by the apparition of
the wild-looking shipwrecked man, the princess
is not afraid : " for Athena put courage in her
heart, and took trembling away from her limbs."
The perfect taste which appears in the Homeric
treatment of the situation implies something beyond and above itself. No poet could have so

imagined that scene whose instincts had not been
moulded by a chivalrous respect for women ; and
no poet could have clothed the image in such language whose own mind was not pure.[1] Nausicaa
shows Odysseus the way to her father's city, by
driving in front of him, while he follows on foot ;
but she directs him to stop at a poplar grove outside the city, lest by entering it in her train he
should give occasion for comment. Alcinous
afterwards blames his daughter for not having
herself conducted the stranger to the house ; and
his words are another proof of the freedom which
respect secured to such a maiden. One last
glimpse of Nausicaa is when Odysseus, in all the
comeliness which Athena has shed over him, is
passing into the banquet-hall, and Nausicaa is
standing at the door ; she says to him : " Fare-
well, stranger, and think of me hereafter, even in
thine own land ; for to me the first thou owest
the price of life." And he answers : " Nausicaa,
daughter of great-hearted Alcinous, yea, may Zeus
the thunderer, the lord of Here, grant me to reach
my home, and see the day of my returning ; so
would I, even there, do worship to thee, as to a
goddess, all my days ; for thou, maiden, hast given
me my life."

[1] There is one verbal trait which curiously illustrates this ;
where Odysseus is described as about to " approach " the maidens, the word employed is one which no Greek poet of a more
sophisticated age would have used in such a context (Od. 6. 136,
μίξεσθαι).

The Homeric women generally are characterized by a gentle dignity and a refinement in which
no modern civilization could show their superiors.
They are essentially feminine, without being in-
sipid or inane ; their sphere is in the home ; their
occupation is in the ministries of wife and mother,
of sister and daughter ; and in everything that
Homer shows us of their relations, we recognize
a natural warmth of domestic affections and a
noble tone of manners.   There are indeed two
Homeric exceptions to such a standard ; but in
each case there are touches which render these
exceptions fresh proofs of the rule.   Nestor refers
to the terrible crime of Agamemnon's wife; but in
doing so he notes how she had yielded only to the
persistence of the tempter Aegisthus : " Verily at
the first the fair Clytaemnestra would have nothing
to do with the foul deed; for she had a good
understanding."   And Helen at least feels a re-
morse which no reproaches could make sharper.
The noble element in her character comes out in
response to nobleness ; it is when her brother-in-
law, Hector, has been vainly striving to inspire
Paris with something of his own generous patriotism, that Helen's self-condemnation breaks forth
in its bitterest utterance.

Thus in the Odyssey there is present the first
condition of a worthy social life ; women are
Tone of social surrounded with the reverence, and ex-
intercourse. ercise the influence, which ought to be
theirs.   And the tone of social intercourse found

in the Odyssey has a corresponding refinement.
If one had to specify its most general characteristic, one might perhaps say that it was the
root of all courtesy, a fine regard for the feelings of others. The behavior of Alcinous, when
he notices that Odysseus is painfully affected by
the minstrel's song, and presently makes an excuse for moving from the banquet-hall, is a case
in point. The same delicacy of feeling marks the
whole scene in the house of Menelaus, when
Helen and he entertain the youthful Telemachus
and his friend, Nestor's son Peisistratus. The
people for whom such poetry was written must
have been a people of naturally acute perceptions :
one feels this all through the social scenes of the
Odyssey. There is nothing in the Athenian literature of the fifth and fourth centuries B. C. which
equals the Odyssey in this particular charm, rich
though Plato's dialogues are in proofs of what cultivated intelligence could do to embellish society.
If we ask the reason, surely it must be sought,
at least to a great extent, in the fact that the
position of women was so much higher, and their
influence so much sounder, in the Homeric age.
The place of Arêtè cannot be supplied by Aspa-
sia. Modern readers are apt to feel that the
Odyssey is more modern than the Iliad. The
chief reason is that, in the domestic scenes of the
Odyssey, they recognize so much which corresponds with modern feeling in regard to the relationships of the family.

Brief as this survey has necessarily been, it will
have indicated in what sense Iliad and
Odyssey alike possess that charm which
we are wont to associate with "the
childhood of the world," — a phrase which may
be unscientific, or even in some degree misleading, but which at least expresses our modern feeling that in these poems there is a freshness, a
simplicity, a beauty, which are altogether beyond
the reach of art ; which, when their natural bloom
is over, can never be artificially renewed ; and
which belong to an age that, in respect of conscious thought, is related to our own as childhood
to maturity.

There is, however, another aspect of Homeric
epos which must also be clearly apprehended. Its
form represents a perfection of poetical art which
must have been gradually attained. Experience
shows that the earliest efforts to employ a language in metrical composition are inseparable from
some degree of rudeness. There is a struggle of
thought with expression, a tendency to ignoble or
grotesque modes of speech, an incapacity for the
equable maintenance of a high level. Homeric
epos bears no such traces of the primitive stage
in literature. It has a perfectly artistic and elastic medium of utterance, which the poet uses with
easy and unfailing mastery. The union of such
consummate art in poetical form with the spiritual
character of a simple age is the unique distinction
of the Homeric poems. And we observe further

*Summary.
General char-
acter of Ho-
meric poetry.*

that the personality of the artist is suppressed. He is to us as Demodocus and Phemius were to the listeners in the Odyssey, merely the prophet of the god, — the inspired man to whom this gift of song has been committed.

Next to Homer early Greek tradition placed another famous poet, recognized as the founder of a characteristic type in epic poetry ; one which was regarded as forming a kind of antithesis to the Homeric. Hesiod figures in legend as Homer's rival. They contended, the story said, at Chalcis in Euboea. Each recited passages from his greatest work : Homer, from the Iliad ; Hesiod, from the Works and Days ; and Hesiod triumphed. Hesiodic epos is represented, for us, by three extant poems, and some fragments. Two of these three poems are, fortunately, those with which Hesiod's name was chiefly associated throughout Hellas ; while the third, though greatly inferior in interest and value to the others, serves at least to illustrate one phase in the later development of the Hesiodic school. These three are, the Works and Days, the Theogony, and the Shield of Heracles.

The poem entitled Works and Days is the most characteristic of Hesiod, and was so regarded by the ancients. In the present text there is some spurious matter, and not a little confusion ; nor can the original form of the composition be exactly determined. Still, the nucleus, at least, is undoubtedly genuine, and bears a stamp which is in striking contrast with the Homeric. It cannot be placed later than the eighth century B. C. In the age of Archilochus, at the beginning of the seventh century B. C., the name of Hesiod was already famous.

The poet had a younger brother, named Perses, who had acquired more than his due share of their common patrimony by bribing certain judges. After living in idleness on this ill-gotten wealth, Perses is now reduced to begging from Hesiod, who declines to give him anything more, except good advice. And the sum of this advice is, " Work, and be just." The first part of the poem is concerned with Perses and the moral reflections which he suggests.

The second part consists of directions concerning the various tasks of the husbandman, and hints of prudence for seafaring men. This is the part from which the poem takes the first half of its title, the *Works*. There is a sort of appendix to it, in about seventy verses, — precepts as to marriage, friendship, and other subjects ; also as to certain ceremonial observances, necessary if one would avoid the displeasure of the gods.

The third and last part teaches what days of the month are lucky or unlucky for certain actions. " Sometimes a day is a stepmother, sometimes a mother." This calendar has suggested the second half of the composite title, Works and *Days*.

When we consider this singular composition

as a whole, the impression which it leaves on
the mind might be described by saying that there
is a foreground and a background. The foreground is held by the definite practical teaching.
The background is formed by Hesiod's general
views of human destiny; and these claim the
first notice. They are gloomy. Four ages of the
world have gone before that into which Hesiod
has been born: the golden age, when men lived
like the gods, with no sickness or sorrow or decay, and died as if subdued by sleep; the silver
age, in which childhood lasted a hundred years,
but the later period of existence was embittered
and shortened by men's own impiety; the age
of bronze, terrible and fierce in its warfare; and
then, as if by a partial return to the better days
of the human race, the age of the heroes, such as
fought at Troy, whose nature was half divine, and
who passed from life to the Islands of the Blest,
by the Ocean stream in the region of the sunset.
And now Hesiod exclaims bitterly: " Would that
I had not to live in the fifth age! Would that I
had died earlier, or that my birth had fallen on
later days! For now there is a race of iron."

It is not clear why he should have wished that
he had been born later; for he adds that the race
of iron will be followed by an age still more de-
praved than itself. What is the origin of evil?
Hesiod has his answer to that question. Zeus
could not forgive Prometheus for having stolen
fire from heaven. He therefore ordered the god

Hephaestus to fashion a beautiful maiden. When she had been made, Athena gave her a girdle and fair robes; the Graces and Persuasion hung golden chains upon her; the Hours crowned her with the flowers of spring; the god Hermes gave her guile and deceiving words: and because every god had dowered her with a gift, she was called the maiden of all gifts, Pandora. Then Zeus sent her to the brother of Prometheus, named, not, like him, from forethought, but from afterthought, — from taking thought when it is too late, — Epimetheus. Epimetheus had been warned by his wiser brother not to accept any gift from Zeus; but he disregarded the advice and received Pandora. This crafty maiden then took the lid off a certain large jar, in which all the evils that now plague the world had been shut up; and those evils went abroad, to be imprisoned nevermore. Only Hope remained under the rim of the jar; for Pandora had replaced the lid before Hope could flutter forth.

And now, in this iron age, wrong-doing is rampant; great men devour bribes and give crooked judgments. "Fools," cries Hesiod, "who know not how much more is the half than the whole, who know not how happily a man may live on mallows and squills!" For the edification of such great men Hesiod tells a fable, an αἶνος, — the earliest specimen of its class in European literature. Thus said the hawk to the nightingale, when he was carrying her through the high clouds in the grip of his talons, and she, transfixed on their sharp points, was wailing piteously, — this was his stern speech to her : " Silly creature, why dost thou scream ? Thou art in the grasp of the stronger; thou shalt go wherever I take thee, songstress though thou art ; I will make a meal of thee, if I please, or I will let thee fall. It is folly to think of striving against one's betters. Then one is vanquished, and adds pain to disgrace."

Hesiod protests earnestly against the hawk's doctrine that might is right. He draws a vivid picture of the blessings that might attend on a city in which justice was respected : "That city thrives, and the people flourish in it ; peace, nurturer of youth, is in the land, and Zeus never ordains grievous warfare for that folk. Hunger and calamity wait not on men who give righteous judgment ; but their fields are glad with festal joys. The earth yields them plenty ; on the mountains, the oak bears acorns aloft and shelters bees beneath ; the sheep are heavy with their burden of fleecy wool ; the women bear children like unto their parents. They enjoy all good things in full measure ; they travel not in ships ; but the graingiving Earth yields them her fruit."

This picture must be understood, not as describing what Hesiod conceived to be possible for his own iron age, but rather as an ideal image of what might have been if the human race, in its downward course, had not angered the gods and increased its own troubles. As matters stand, "the gods have hidden the means of life from men." Hard, unremitting toil is man's portion; all his industry, all his foresight, all his scrupulous attention to signs and omens, are demanded, if he is to escape dire poverty, dire suffering, and premature death.

Such is the general view of life which forms the gloomy background of Hesiod's poem. But when we turn to the practical teaching which fills the foreground, we find ourselves amidst comparatively cheerful surroundings. If there is nothing brilliant or beautiful or generous, at least there is the stir of busy work, and the fresh, open-air feeling of a close communion with the varying sights and sounds of the fields at each season of the year. A few lines from the beginning of the precepts on farming will serve to give some idea of the style: "When the Pleiads, the daughters of Atlas, rise, begin thy reaping; but thy ploughing, when they are about to set. Forty nights and forty days are they hidden, but re-appear as the seasons come round, when the sickle is first sharpened. That is the rule of the fields for men, whether they dwell by the sea, or in the hollows of valleys far from the surging deep. Strip off thy coat when thou sowest, when thou ploughest, when thou reapest, if thou wouldst gather in all thy fruits in their season; lest perchance thou fall on a mid-time of poverty, and go begging to other men's houses, and get nothing: as thou,

Perses, hast now come to me ; but verily I will give thee no more, nor replenish thy measure. Work, foolish Perses ; work the works that the gods have set for men."

Hesiod insists, as might have been expected, on the virtue of early rising : "Morning claims a third part of the day's work ; morning sets us forward on a journey or on a task, — morning, who at her coming puts many men on the road, and lays the yoke on many oxen." And one of the charms of the poem is that it so often breathes the breath of those early morning hours when, in winter, the poet saw the mists resting on the tilled lands of wealthy Boeotian farmers, and saw it gladly, because such mists are kindly to the wheat crop ; or when, as spring came on, he looked in the pale light over a landscape tinted by the early shoots of fig-tree and vine, which he has in mind when he speaks of the "gray" spring, or caught the note of some bird that marked a critical moment in his busy calendar. "Give heed when thou hearest the voice of the crane from the clouds overhead, as she utters her cry from year to year. Her voice gives the sign for ploughing, and proclaims the season of rainy winter, and pierces the heart of the man who has not provided himself with oxen. It is easy to say, 'Lend me a pair of oxen and a wagon ;' but it is also easy to answer, 'Nay, my oxen are busy.'" The swallow, heard at daybreak, warns the husbandman that the early spring pruning of

the vines must be delayed no longer.   And as
spring is passing into early summer, the farmer
who has deferred his ploughing knows that his last
opportunity has come " when the cuckoo utters
her cry from amid the leaves and gladdens the
hearts of men the wide world over."   The smaller
signs which the poet notes are often curious.
When snails leave the ground and begin to crawl
over plants, this shows that the summer season is
too far advanced to permit further labor at the
vines ; it is time to prepare for the early harvest.
A good rainfall in spring is such as fills, but only
fills, the prints made by the hoofs of the oxen.
The spring season for navigation has arrived when
the leaves on the upper branches of the fig-tree
have unfolded to about the length of a crow's foot-
print.

Hesiod's warnings against laziness or procrasti-
nation are often couched in pithy sayings which
have the flavor of rustic proverbs.   In wintry
weather a man must not be tempted to waste his
time by gossiping in the warm forge, lest afterwards he " press a swollen foot with a lean hand ; "
that is, suffer from that twofold effect of starva-
tion.   The importance of storing up grain is en-
forced by the words, " Drive the spiders out of
your jars."   A sharp north wind is graphically
described as one which " makes an old man trot."
" Take your fill from your wine-jar when it is full
and when it is low, but spare it halfway down ;
thrift in the dregs is a poor thing."   The maxims

on the conduct of life in general are of the same
type, and evince rustic caution of a somewhat
cynical type; many of them, too, bear the stamp
of life in an isolated hamlet, where a man's comfort depends much on having good relations with
his few neighbors. "Invite your well-wisher to
dinner, and let your enemy alone; but especially
invite your neighbor." The reason for the last
clause is given directly: "If any mishap should
occur in the village, your neighbors come without
stopping to make their toilet;" but those who
are further off, even though kinsfolk, stop to
make it. "Men have been ruined by trusting,
and by mistrusting." "Do not make any friend
as close as a brother." "If you do, then take
care not to provoke him by injury; but if he
wrongs you by word or deed, remember it, and
requite him doubly. If he once more makes
overtures of friendship, and is willing to render
satisfaction, meet him halfway." "Smilingly demand a witness from your own brother;" that is,
do not believe your own brother on his mere
word, but at the same time appear to be playful,
and pretend that you desire the witness merely
because it is more businesslike. The advice re-
specting marriage is equally circumspect. The
poet is not a misogynist, but the chief characteristic of his attitude towards the female sex is
caution. A man should choose a wife among his
neighbors, says Hesiod, after a very careful survey; else his choice may supply these same

neighbors with matter of animadversion.   He
admits, indeed, though somewhat dryly, that there
is nothing better than a good wife.

All this is in the tone of the Boeotian farmer :
how far we have traveled from the world of the
Homeric Arêtè and Nausicaa !   The poet of the
Works and Days has a hard head and a not very
generous heart ; his cold and cautious prudence
is often sordid.   Even the duty of propitiating
the gods by worship is referred to a mercenary
motive, — " that thou mayest buy another man's
land, instead of his buying thine."   Yet along
with so much that is hard or ignoble there is at
least one element of nobleness, — a real feeling for
the dignity of work.   " Work is no reproach ; the
reproach is to be idle."   And there is the feeling,
too, that work makes for righteousness ; work belongs to the divine scheme for men, and it is the
idle man who becomes unjust.   Thus the lower
side of the poet's teaching is qualified by such
sentiments as this : " It is easy to find wicked-
ness abundantly ; the path is smooth and short.
But the immortals have decreed that only toil
shall reach Virtue.   Long and steep is the way to
her, and rough at the first ; but when the higher
ground is reached, difficult though the path be, it
is less difficult thenceforth."

From the Works and Days we pass to the second poem by which Hesiod is chiefly
represented, the Theogony.   Here we
are told how Earth arose out of chaos ; how the

The Theo-
gony.

eldest dynasty of gods, the first-born of the ele-
mental powers, was overthrown by the younger
dynasty of Zeus; and how each person of the
Olympian hierarchy came into being. What is
there in common, it might be asked, between such
a theme and a body of practical rules, like that
contained in the Works and Days, for the conduct
of daily life? How are we to conceive the basis,
the fundamental idea, of the Hesiodic school, if
these two poems are alike characteristic of it?
The Theogony itself supplies the answer. It is
not, in the Homeric sense, a work of art. Such
unity as it possesses is derived from the thread of
divine genealogy. It is a compilation of current
lore concerning the parentage and relationships of
the deities; the object being to give this lore in
a continuous form. The work has been skilfully
done; and the essential dryness of the subject has
been occasionally relieved by short episodes. One
of these, the battle of the gods and Titans, imitates the style of the Iliad; though it may be
doubted whether this passage belonged to the
earliest form of the composition. The poem remained a standard authority. Herodotus couples
Hesiod with Homer as a creator of the Greek theogony. The Homeric poetry prevailed by its own
charm; the Hesiodic poem, which is little more
than an Olympian peerage, could prevail only by
authority. What was that authority? It is only
a conjecture, though a plausible one, that the Theogony had the sanction of Delphi. Its materials

must have been largely derived from temple-legends, often inconsistent with each other ; and the compiler's endeavor to harmonize them could not easily have succeeded if the priesthood of Apollo had withheld the seal of their approval. In this connection it is interesting to note a few points of contact between the language of Delphi and the language of Hesiod.   The μέγα νήπιε Πέρση of the Works and Days has an echo in the μέγα νήπιε Κροῖσε of the Delphic oracle (Her. 1. 85).   That oracle often used enigmatic substitutes for common words, as when rivers were called by it "drainers of the hills" (ὀρεμπόται). This trait is strongly marked in Hesiod, as when he calls the snail the "house-carrier" (φερέοικος).   And a verse from the Works and Days (285) actually occurs in a response given at Delphi (Her. 6. 86).

We see, then, that the basis common to the two chief Hesiodic poems, the Works and Days and the Theogony, is the practical tendency : in the one case, to direct the farmer's daily life ; in the other, to produce an orthodox history of the gods which should be useful as a standard work of reference. In neither case is the play of imagination altogether excluded, but the practical purpose predominates ; the poet's first object is to instruct ; whereas in poetry such as the Homeric, of which the aim is ideal, the first object is delight.

The Shield of Heracles.   The third poem which bears the name of Hesiod is certainly much later than the age to which the two others must be re-

ferred, — the short epic called the Shield of Heracles. Other miniature epics of the same general
class were also ascribed to Hesiod. What, it may
be asked, is the distinctively Hesiodic feature in
such compositions? Is not the Shield, in subject
and in form, rather Homeric than Hesiodic? Our
materials for an answer are scanty. But it may be
suggested that the work of the Hesiodic school in
this kind set out, originally at least, from the same
point of view as the Theogony, namely, from the
desire to preserve the facts of local legend. The
purpose was less poetical than historical. Gradually, it may be, the Hesiodic poetry became, in
this province, a direct imitation of the Homeric;
and that is certainly the phase which the Shield
of Heracles seems to represent.

The broad differences between the style of
Hesiod and that of Homer correspond Style of He-
with the inner difference of spirit. Ho- siod — compared with
mer's directness of thought and sim- the Homeric.
plicity of language are always joined to nobleness.
In the Works and Days Hesiod's thoughts are
generally plain, and his language also; but his
style is not always noble; it is often too homely
for that; and, with or without homeliness, it is
often quaint. One form of such quaintness is the
device already mentioned as oracular, of riddling
synonyms for plain words. Thus the hand is
called "the five-branched" (πέντοζος); a thief is
"one who sleeps by day" (ἡμερόκοιτος). Homer
speaks of "swift ships, which are the horses of

the sea for men;" Hesiod would not have scru-
pled to use the phrase "horses of the sea" as a
substitute for the word "ships," leaving his meaning to be guessed. Again, Hesiod is rapid only
in so far as the natural lightness of the Greek
hexameter profits all who use it. He is not rapid
in the further and higher sense in which Homer
is so, — by virtue of the impetuous thought which
is always darting onwards. Hesiod does not
sweep us along on a swift flow of verse. He is
usually concise, pointed, emphatic. Each fact or
precept is stated tersely, in the manner which he
thinks fitted to fix it in the mind; and then he
goes on to his next fact. He hardly cares to
provide smooth transitions, or to give his series
of facts a fluent continuity. His small groups of
verses are rather like so many separate beads on
a string. If such verses were recited, they would
not hold listeners as the Homeric poetry does.
They are meant rather to sink into the mind of
the individual who shall ponder them as he toils
in the fields or wends his way to the temple.

Lastly, the Hesiodic poet is utterly unlike the
Homeric in this, that he does not sup-
press himself. The artist merges his
personality in his work. A teacher such as Hesiod cannot do so. He comes forward as an expounder of lore, religious, moral, or technical: the
force of the message depends not a little on the
personal earnestness of the prophet. The verses
prefixed to the Theogony, in which Hesiod de-

Hesiod as a teacher.

scribes how the Muses appeared to him when
he was keeping his sheep on Helicon, may be of
another origin from the poem itself; but the
words there ascribed to the Muses happily sum
up the difference between Homeric and Hesiodic
epos. "We know," they say, "how to tell fables
that seem like realities, and we know also, when
we choose, how to relate true things." "To relate true things" was the distinctive bent of Hesiodic poetry. It represents the effort to adapt the
form of Ionian epos to a different genius and to
material of a different order. This effort had
only a limited success. The literary interest of
the Hesiodic poetry is indeed manifold; but Greek
epos, as a characteristic expression of the Greek
spirit, is represented by Homer, and by Homer
alone.

The true instinct of the Asiatic Ionians created
new forms for new material, so soon as they became conscious that they had outlived the great
age of their own epic poetry. And in Greece
proper, also, new forms were developed. To trace
the earlier course of that development will be the
aim of the next lecture.

GREEK LYRIC POETRY: THE COURSE OF ITS DE-VELOPMENT

THE epic was for long the only poetry, artistic in form, which the Greeks possessed. If a lower limit for the period be sought, it may be placed approximately at the close of the eighth century B. C. Till then epos held a solitary supremacy; and the secret of the spell which it exerted was in the charm of the past. The listeners surrendered themselves to the magic of a flowing narrative which carried them into an ideal region of heroic life,—not the life of the present, and yet linked with it by the simple faith of the men for whom the minstrel recited. Their own interests and thoughts seldom ranged beyond the sphere of action in which the heroes moved, and the sphere of debate or social intercourse in which the minds of the heroes found utterance. But gradually a change came. Monarchies gave place to oligarchies, and these to tyrannies, or lastly to democracies. Hellenic life became fuller of experiences and efforts which stimulated the thoughts of the individual, — giving him new tasks, new objects of ambition, new possibilities of enjoyment. This was more especially the case in the Ionian colonies of Asia

Conditions which required new forms of poetry.

Minor. Their cities were in the neighborhood of
barbarian foes; they were drawn together by the
need of mutual protection; their social qualities,
and their consciousness of the higher differences
between Greek and barbarian, were thus quickened. Above all, familiarity with the most re-
pellent aspects of Oriental despotism served to
strengthen in them the Hellenic love of freedom.
The Asiatic Ionians were the first
Greeks among whom democratic insti- The Ionians
tutions ripened, however imperfectly. Minor.
They were also the first among whom a life of
some cultivation and refinement became possible
for large classes of the citizens. The century
from 750 to 650 B. C. saw the beginning of this
change. It was also a period of enterprise and
discovery. Distant seas and lands were explored;
colonies were founded; commerce became more
active; the bounds of knowledge were enlarged
in many directions, and reflection was stimulated.

The new poetry corresponded to this new state
of things. It was the voice of the individual
man, interested in the present, and desirous of
expressing his own thoughts among his friends.
It took two forms, those known as the Elegiac and
the Iambic. They must be considered separately,
and we will begin with the Elegiac.

The word *elegos*, "elegy," was proba- Elegiac
bly of Armenian origin, meaning first origin. Its
a misfortune, a sad event, and then a kind of
dirge, played on the flute, for the dead. Phrygia

was the region in which the music of the flute
was first developed, especially by the musical reformer Olympus, in the eighth century B. C.
From Phrygia the word *elegos* came to the Ionian
Greeks on the coasts of Asia Minor. Greek poets
now set Greek words to this mournful flute dirge,
which in its original form had been instrumental
only. The earliest Greek elegies were doubtless
purely lyric,— short mournful songs. Flute music,
however, was not funereal only : in Ionia it became popular at social gatherings ; and it could
also appeal in stirring strains to the warlike spirit.
Hence by the side of the funeral elegy other
kinds arose. A poem of some length addressed
to a gathering of friends, or intended for the citizens at large, could be recited after the epic
fashion, being introduced by singing a few verses
to the flute music, and concluded in a similarly
lyric manner. Such elegies, mainly recited, but
prefaced and closed by singing, were now couched
The elegiac   in the metre known as the elegiac coup-
couplet.
           let. The Greek word for this couplet,
elegion, was naturally of later origin than the word
elegos ; it occurs first in Attic writers of the fifth
century B. C. This couplet was the invention of
Ionian poets familiar with the epic hexameter.
The hexameter obviously required modification
before it could be adapted to the requirements of
the new poetry. Hesiod could use the hexameter
as a vehicle for his precepts, even on homely
themes, because he maintained the tone of an in-

spired teacher. But the confidences of friend to friend, or the exhortations of citizen to fellow-citizens, could not appropriately wear such a garb. Epic verse was too stately for that purpose. And it was open to a further objection. It was ill suited to those shorter effusions which the new poetry encouraged. If the flow of heroic verse is to have its proper effect, that flow must not be confined within too narrow limits. On the other hand, the unit of the heroic measure, the hexameter, had been inseparably associated by long use with the very idea of artistic poetry.

Such considerations determined the choice of the first instrument adopted by the new poetry. The hexameter was retained ; but to each such verse was added a curtailed hexameter, the so-called pentameter. The pair forms a couplet to which the cadence of the second verse gives a natural close. Hence even a single elegiac couplet has the effect of a complete whole. The elegiac couplet has a further characteristic which illustrates the history of elegiac poetry. Homeric epos had shown the capacity of the hexameter to express the most diverse feelings, — wrath, scorn, fear, entreaty, pity, anguish, tenderness. It could be modulated with almost endless variety. In the elegiac couplet it is the first verse, the hexameter, which pitches the tone of feeling ; and the hexameter brings all its inherent versatility to the new metre. The relation of the second verse, the pentameter, to the first is again infinitely various.

If the hexameter has been a trumpet-call to battle,
the pentameter, by its gentler tone, can give an
effect of contrast. Or if the first verse has been
pathetic, the second verse can echo it in a softer
key. Universally, the effect of the pentameter in
the elegiac couplet is that, instead of sweeping the
mind onward, as is done by a continuous flow of
hexameter verse, it invites our thought to return
upon itself ; it gives a meditative pause, a moment
of reflection. And these two essential properties
of the elegiac couplet are expressed in the actual
course of the elegiac development. Elegiac poetry was universal in its range of theme ; but its
tone was always tinged with meditation, and often
with sadness.

The varied capabilities of elegy are sufficiently
displayed by the series of poets who represent it during the first two centuries
or so of its existence, the period in
which it was freshest and most vigorous, from
about 700 B. C. down to the time of the Persian
wars. The fragments which remain are indeed for
the most part meagre, but they illustrate the
wide range of tones which the new instrument
could yield. Callīnus of Ephesus, the
earliest elegist on record, belonging to
the first decades of the seventh century, appears,
in the few verses which remain, as the author of
a stirring appeal to the warlike spirit which had
too long slumbered in the bosoms of his Ionian
fellow-citizens, now menaced by the invasion of a

Elegiac poets, and their themes.

Callīnus.

barbarian horde. Martial elegy soon has another
representative in another Ionian, Tyrtaeus, who found more congenial listen- _Tyrtaeus._
ers in the youth of Sparta, his adopted home.
Alike in technical skill and in manly vigor, Tyr
taeus is greatly superior to Callīnus. In some of
his couplets the call to battle rings out like a clar-
ion note. Meanwhile, a greater poet than either
Callīnus or Tyrtaeus had been illustrating the primary use of elegy in lament for the dead. From
the Ionian Archilochus of Paros we have
some beautiful verses mourning the fate _Archilochus._
of friends who had been lost at sea. Somewhat
later, but before the close of the seventh century,
Mimnermus of Smyrna strikes yet an-
other note. He composed martial ele- _Mimnermus._
gies, among others; but his distinction is that of
being the first elegiac poet known to us who applied elegy to themes of love. His tone is plain-
tive, and marked by the inevitable sadness of one
who prizes life only for those pleasures which old
age takes away. He is indeed the interpreter of
a degenerating Ionia, of a people destined to bear
the yoke; but he is also interesting as the poetical ancestor of those elegiac poets, Greek or
Roman, whose chief inspiration was derived from
tender sentiment.

With Solon, at the beginning of the sixth century, a new element comes into elegy.
He employs it for the utterance of his _Solon._
thoughts on the evils which afflict Attica, and on

his own efforts to remedy them. These are the
thoughts of a statesman who is also a philosopher;
they are inseparably connected with still wider
and deeper reflections on the permanent conditions
of human life. Man proposes, but the gods dis-
pose; the prophet can read omens, but cannot
avert fate; the physician can prescribe, but has
no assurance of healing. Solon thus represents
in its highest form that tendency of Greek elegy
which is described by the term "gnomic," — the
desire to inculcate moral precepts and practical
wisdom. This tendency was continued, though in
a feebler and more prosaic strain, by
Phocylides of Miletus, who belonged to
the second half of the sixth century. And at the
same period it found a more interesting exponent
in Theognis of Megara, the only Dorian,
perhaps, who attained eminence in elegiac poetry. Theognis, an aristocrat impoverished
and exiled by the triumph of the democratic party
in his native Megara, is a man to whom the world
is out of joint, but whose faith in the beliefs and
traditions of Dorian aristocracy is unshaken. That
faith is as inseparable from his belief in the divine
government of the world as the royalism of a
French emigrant in the days of the Revolution
was inseparable from his Catholicism; when the
Dorian aristocracy is depressed, the face of heaven
is darkened : but even in that twilight of the gods
Theognis still sacrifices to the goddess Hope; and
meanwhile he is fain to impress salutary counsels

Phocylides.

Theognis.

on his young friend Cyrnus. There is at once a
kinship and a contrast between the elegiac moral-
ist, who thus enforces traditional maxims, and the
philosopher Xenophanes, who towards
the close of the sixth century used elegy Xenophanes.
in protest against certain usages of his day. Xenophanes is anxious to raise the tone of conversation
at dinner-parties, where the guests were too much
addicted to entertaining each other with the fic-
tions of the old poets. He would fain have them
turn from Centaurs and Titans to more edifying
topics. Again, he deprecates the honor paid to
athletes, while men of intellect are neglected.
This last view, put forward about the time when
great lyrists were writing odes of victory, stamps
Xenophanes as a man thoroughly out of accord
with ordinary Hellenic life; in his hands, elegy
gave one more proof of its versatility by serving
the purpose of the modern pamphlet, in which
a social reformer airs his favorite crotchet. We
now come to the age of the Persian
wars; and Simonides shows how the ele- Simonides.
giac couplet can be made a vehicle for commem-
orative inscription, — summing up great national
events in a few clear - cut words, beautiful as
sculpture, or finding an utterance for public or
private grief. Sappho had already given an exquisite example of elegiac pathos in her epitaph
of four lines on the maiden Timas. But no one
before or after Simonides illustrated as he did the
full efficacy of the elegiac metre for every kind of

monumental expression. Take, for instance, those
four simple lines on the men of Tegea who had
fallen in war, — probably in the battle of Plataea
(fr. 102, Bergk) : —

τῶνδε δι' ἀνθρώπων ἀρετὰν οὐχ ἵκετο καπνὸς
αἰθέρα, δαιομένης εὐρυχόρου Τεγέης·
οἳ βούλοντο πόλιν μὲν ἐλευθερίᾳ τεθαλυῖαν
παισὶ λιπεῖν, αὐτοὶ δ' ἐν προμάχοισι πεσεῖν.

" It was due to the valor of these men that smoke
did not go up to heaven from the burning of spacious
Tegea.   Their choice was to leave their children a city
flourishing in freedom, and to lay down their own lives
in the front of the battle."

Observe the noble and massive simplicity of the
words, which follow each other in a perfectly natural order ; the force with which the first couplet
describes the greatness of the peril, and the simple pathos with which the second describes the
resolve by which that peril was averted.

Elegiac poetry thus afforded a field in which any
Popular   man could try his poetical powers on
character of
elegiac poetry. any theme.   Other forms, the epic, the
lyric, the dramatic, were bound by traditions re-
quiring a certain correspondence between form
and subject - matter ; they were also connected
with certain divisions of the Greek race, as the
choral lyric was especially Dorian, and as Tragedy
was Attic.   But elegy was entirely free in regard
to range of subject-matter, and was open to all.
And no other form of Greek poetry had so pro-

longed an existence. From 700 B. C. down to the
fall of the Eastern Empire, verse continued to be written in the elegiac metre. Its enduring
vitality.
Constantinus Cephalas was adding recent work
to his Anthology at the time when the English
Æthelstan was defeating the Danes. Out of some
2,800 epigrams in the Palatine collection, all but
about 300 are elegiac. This enduring popularity
of the elegiac measure was due to the fact that it
was so tolerant of mediocrity. Before Herodotus,
the Greeks had nothing that can properly be called
prose literature. The elegiac form of poetry partly
supplied that defect. If the remains of the early
elegists are so scanty, one reason may be that
their work was so abundant and so unequal. It
was welcome as a familiar companion to Greeks
of an age when poetry was judged by the higher
standards of art ; but it was also less likely to be
preserved. We take more care of a book than of
a newspaper. The great bulk of extant Greek
elegy dates from an age when the creative prime
of the Greek genius was over.

Iambic poetry comes into view at the same
period as elegiac ; that is, at the beginning of the seventh century. While Iambic
poetry.
the elegiac form was a modification of the stately
epic, the iambic starts from the opposite pole.
To the Greeks it seemed the nearest of all metres
to the cadence of every-day speech. Aristotle
observes that people were apt to make undesigned
iambic rhythms in speaking, and the texts of the

orators illustrate his remark. The origin of the
Obscurity of its origin. name and of the rhythm is obscure.
Greek legend pointed to an early use of
some iambic measure in that popular jesting, of
a satirical kind, which custom licensed at certain
festivals. When Demeter was mourning for her
daughter, the first smile was drawn from her, it
was said, by the sallies of the maid Iambè. The
very old comic poem Margites is known to have
mingled iambic verses with hexameters. But the
origin of the iambic rhythm, and of the closely
kindred trochaic, was perhaps not Hellenic. The
word *iambus* is conjecturally traced to Phrygia;
and it is noteworthy that a town called Iambus,
near the Troad, is mentioned by Hesychius. The
Phrygian founder of the improved flute music,
Olympus, is said to have composed in iambic and
trochaic rhythms. The trochee was used in songs
belonging to the early ritual of Dionysus, which
came into Thrace from Phrygia. The Ionians,
the first Greeks who used these rhythms, may
have derived them partly from Phrygia, partly from
Thrace.

Both these regions were known to the Ionian
Archilochus. poet who, early in the seventh century,
artistically developed those rhythms,
Archilochus of Paros. He wrote iambic or trochaic verses of various lengths, and combined
these with dactylic or other metres. For poems
composed in these measures he probably used
two different modes of delivery. One of these

modes was purely lyric, the verses being sung
throughout. In the other mode, the beginning
and end of the poem were sung, while the middle part of it was given in recitative, with a musical accompaniment. His poems in the iambic
or trochaic measure were designed to be recited
among friends at social gatherings, as elegiac
poems often were.

The iambic form, as used by Archilochus, was
associated with fierce personal satire. Iambic satire.
His younger contemporary, Simonides Simonides of
of Amorgus, also applied it to satire, Amorgus.
though rather general than personal. Hippônax.
And about a century later, Hippônax of Ephesus
once more used iambic verse as a weapon of personal attack, giving the verse that peculiarly un-
graceful form known as the scazon, or "limping."
Thus within a hundred and fifty years we find
three Ionians who use the metre in satire. Its
fitness for the purpose depended prima- Why iambics
rily on its nearness to the rhythm of were so used.
common speech. This made it a fitting metre in
which to deal with those ludicrous or sordid aspects of life and character for which the elegiac
measure, with its epic affinities, was too noble and
too gentle. The old legends of the suicides caused
by the early Ionian satirists may or may not be
founded on fact, but in any case they are suggestive.
We cannot tell whether Archilochus really drove
Neobulè and her kinsfolk to self-destruction, or
whether Hippônax had the same effect on the

sculptor Bupalus. But the general credence which
the ancients gave to such stories proves the scath-
ing force which they must have felt in the satires,
when they heard or read them.

This side of the iambic tradition was continued
in Attic Comedy. But there is a larger aspect of
iambic poetry which must not be forgotten. The
satirical application, however frequent and characteristic, was after all accidental. It was merely
one particular bent given to the general
faculty of the iambic metre, which was
that of expressing thoughts in a form
relatively near to the ordinary idiom of conversation. The fragments of Archilochus himself suffice to show that he was far from restricting his
new measures to the satirical use. The splendid
trochaic verses addressed to his own troubled soul
do not imply any satirical context. Simonides of
Amorgus also has left us some iambic verses,
moralizing on the evils of human life, which contain nothing that might not with equal propriety
have been said in the elegiac form. Solon's iambics, again, have some themes in common with his
elegiacs. Yet there is also a difference
which should be noted. The elegiac
measure, derived from the epic, suggests
that the poet, like the old minstrel, is addressing
a circle of listeners. Even when he speaks osten-
sibly to one person only, as Theognis to Cyrnus,
the tone is still frankly social ; the things said are
such as might be said in a gathering of friends.

The general character of iambic verse.

How differing from the elegiac.

The iambic form, on the other hand, being more colloquial, is more suitable than the elegiac when the thing to be said is more personal or confiden-tial. Solon illustrates this difference. Both in elegiacs and in iambics Solon re-fers to the troubles of Attica, and to the remedies which he sought for them. In his elegiacs he de-scribes the general character of these remedies. But the iambic form is that which he prefers when he wishes to defend himself in detail, — to answer the taunt that he had shown a shallow understanding or an irresolute spirit by failing to snatch the prizes that were within his grasp, or to meet the complaint 'that he had shipwrecked the hopes of his followers. Such controversy de-manded some approach to the tone of real debate, to the briskness of attack and retort ; and for this the iambic form was the right one. In this gen-eral aspect the iambic tradition was developed by the dialogue of Attic Tragedy.

Illustration from Solon.

When this distinction has been duly noted, the fact remains that elegiac and iambic poetry are essentially companion forms, alike characteristic of the period which immediately followed the age of the great epos. They are companions, because both alike enabled a man to utter what he thought and felt on any subject, public or private, and because neither form made, of necessity, any high demand on the poetical gifts of the person who used it. Of the two, iambic verse required perhaps the higher

Kinship be-tween elegiac and iambic verse.

technical skill ; and that is one reason why it was less popular than the elegiac.

This seems the right place in which to say a few words on the question whether these Grounds for classing them as lyric. two companion forms of poetry should or should not be classed as " lyric." In their origin both were lyric, as we have seen. Certain elegiac and iambic poems were sung throughout, while others at least began and ended with singing. But this connection with music was gradually relaxed, or even lost. In the fifth century B. C., or from a somewhat earlier date, simple recitation, without music, was probably the rule, both for elegiac and for iambic poems. Greeks of the fifth century B. C. called lyric poems *melē* (μέλη). They never applied that term to purely elegiac or purely iambic poetry. These they would have classed, like epic poetry, under the general term *epē* (ἔπη). It would be confusing, then, to describe elegiac and iambic poetry by the Greek term "melic." But there is no objection to describing them as "lyric," if only it be remembered that the justification for doing so is historical ; that is, these forms of poetry were originally lyric, though they afterwards ceased to be so.[1]

---

[1] Bergk calls them lyric, but defends the classification on a ground which seems unsatisfactory, namely, because they are subjective, and thus share the essence of lyric poetry. Greek lyric poetry was not, however, always subjective ; neither was elegiac. Nor in any case ought the word "lyric" to be used as a mere synonym for "subjective." Bergk seems, then, to have taken the right course, but for a questionable reason.

The earlier history of Greek literature is in
one respect not unlike the progress of the Iliad.
When Diomedes has displayed his prowess, it becomes the turn of Ajax, and then of Patroclus,
Menelaus, Achilles. So, in the field of poetry, first
one division of the Greek race, and then another,
comes to the front. The Ionians, after maturing
the epic form, develop the elegiac and the iambic; then Aeolians share with Dorians the glory
of creating lyric poetry; and as the last named
reaches the summit of its excellence, the Athenians are perfecting the drama.

The period during which Greek lyric poetry
flourished is roughly measured by the
two centuries from 650 to 450 B. C. Period of Greek lyric poetry.
No loss which the modern world has
suffered in respect to ancient literature has been
more often deplored than that of the Greek song
to which those centuries gave birth. Of all the
manifold forms which the Greek lyric assumed,
there is only one which is known to us with any
completeness, namely, the ode of victory, as treated
by Pindar. The other forms are represented only
by small fragments. Some of these fragments
are, indeed, inestimable; but relatively to the
body of Greek lyric poetry which the ancients
possessed, the whole collection is a mere handful
of gold-dust. Nine lyric poets, including Pindar,
were recognized by the Alexandrian critics as
standing in the first rank. With the exception of
Pindar himself, there is not one of these whose

work can now be adequately estimated. Even,
however, if the lyric texts had survived, they
could not have been thoroughly appreciated without a more precise knowledge of the music to
which they were set; and if the music, too, had
come down to us, there would still have been a
defect in our comprehension, so far as the choral
lyrics are concerned, since the dancing which
accompanied them was itself a work of elaborate
art.

Nevertheless, this chapter in the literary history of Greece is not a blank. A study of the
fragments, and of scattered notices in ancient literature, has made it possible to trace the general
course of the lyric development, and to recognize
at least the distinctive characteristics of the chief
lyric poets. Greek lyric poetry had two main
Its two main branches. branches, the Aeolian and the Dorian.
The Aeolian lyric was meant to be
sung by a single voice, — it was "monodic;" and
it was essentially the utterance of the singer's
own feelings. The Dorian lyric was choral, and
dealt largely, though not exclusively, with themes
of public interest, especially with those suggested
by public worship. The Dorian lyric was a little
earlier in attaining an artistic form; but it will be
convenient to speak first of the Aeolian.

The Aeolian island of Lesbos was the place
The Aeolian lyric. where the Greek cultivation of music
first made a notable advance. The
Lesbian Terpander (710 B. C.) improved the

four-stringed lyre into an instrument with seven strings, adequate to the purposes of lyric poetry, and may be regarded as practi- Terpander. cally the founder of Greek vocal music. He estab- lished in Lesbos a school of citharodes, "singers to the cithara," which was long famous. The first condition of lyric poetry had thus been cre- ated. The special form which it took in Lesbos was due to the Aeolian temperament, and to the circumstances of the island. Aeolians were char- acterized, above other portions of the Greek race, by vehemence of feeling; they were also sen- suous; but in the higher embodiments of the Aeolian character this sensuousness was ennobled by generous ardor, and refined by an educated instinct for grace and beauty. Lesbos, in the sev- enth century B. C., was a place where every charm of nature and of art coexisted with a large mea- sure of Asiatic opulence. The ruling class was a high-spirited aristocracy, chivalrous and warlike, but also luxurious, and peculiarly appreciative of natural loveliness in every form. Sappho's period of poetical activity belonged to the years Sappho. from about 610 to 570 B. C. From the mass of fiction or calumny which later literature, and especially Attic Comedy, wove around her name only a few leading facts can be disengaged. She was the head of a school or group of pupils in Lesbos, — maidens whom she trained in the lyric art, sometimes with a view to their taking part in the religious festivals. The motives of her poems were usually connected with this circle of disciples, and with the events of their lives. For example, the stanzas beginning φαίνεταί μοι κῆνος refer, it is conjectured, to the man to whom one of her disciples was betrothed. The bridal songs which Sappho composed were again for these young friends. There seem to have been rival teachers in Lesbos, such as Gorgo and Andromeda. Sappho was married, and had a daughter to whom she was devoted. In the political troubles of the island she was driven into exile about 595 B. C., and visited Sicily, but returned to Lesbos about 580. The fragments of her poetry are unique, both for their wonderful melody and for the intensity of passion which the musical words express. They also show the finest sense of beauty in the natural world: in the night sky, when the stars pale before the full moon; or in places where cool streams are shadowed by fruit-trees, and "slumber is shed" on weary eyelids "from the rustling leaves."

The fragments of Sappho, and they alone, reveal the secret of Aeolian poetry at its highest. Nothing that remains from her contemporary, Alcaeus, is of comparable significance. The scanty fragments suffice, indeed, to show his original power in language and in metre. The stanza known as "Sapphic" was his invention, no less than the stanza which bears his own name. For the rest, he is the Lesbian noble whose fiery Aeolian heart was tried by party warfare and

Alcaeus.

by exile, as it was cheered by love and by revelry;
a brilliant cavalier, proud of his own order, who
took the dark days with the bright, — always
ready, like Lovelace, to crown his head with roses
and to drown his cares in the wine-bowl. We
see in him those common elements of Aeolian
character which were clarified in the loftier and
subtler genius of Sappho.

It was no accident that a four-line stanza was
the form of composition principally used
by both these foremost representatives The Aeolian
four-line
of the Aeolian school. Such a stanza, stanza.
repeated without variation, suited the purpose of
their poetry, which was to be sung by one voice,
in social gatherings; just as the massive structure
of the Dorian ode, with its strophe, antistrophe,
and epode, was adapted to choral performance.

After Sappho and Alcaeus, the Aeolian lyric
school found no exponent of similar celebrity.
Little is known, unfortunately, of Sappho's friend
and contemporary, the poetess Erinna, who seems
to have given promise of great excellence before
she died at the age of nineteen; still less is known
of another who belonged to Sappho's circle, Damo-
phyla. But the Aeolian influence reappears in
other combinations. Anacreon, the poet
of courtly festivity, is Aeolian, after the Anacreon.
manner of Alcaeus, in so far as love and revelry
are his themes. But while the strains of Alcaeus
were dignified by ardent feeling and manly spirit,
the Ionian poet's sensuousness is tempered merely

by intellectual grace. The fragments of Anacreon
indicate no passion ; he seems scarcely even in earnest about his pleasures. The soul of the Aeolian
lyric was given to it by the Aeolian genius, and
could not live outside the sphere of Aeolian life.

The claim of the Dorians to the choral lyric
The Dorian
choral lyric. poetry known as Dorian is of a different and a more limited kind. It con-
sists in this, that Dorian public life supplied the
themes with which that poetry was primarily concerned, and also determined that its form should
be choral. But the poets who worked out the
conceptions thus imposed by Dorian life were seldom of Dorian birth. In relation to lyric poetry,
Sparta. Sparta may be regarded as representative of the Dorian influence. It was at
Sparta that the musical improvements of Terpander and his successor, Thaletas, were brought into
harmony with the Cretan art of festal dancing, and
with the forms of lyric composition which Dorian
festivals demanded. The Aeolian singers had
Themes which
Sparta
suggested to a
poet. taken their themes from the emotions
and interests of the individual. But the
Spartan citizen, a soldier in a permanent
camp, was less accustomed to the indulgence of
private sentiment. The feelings most familiar to
the Spartan were those which he shared with all
his civic comrades, gathered for athletic games, or
marshalled for battle, or assembled at the festivals
of the Carneian Apollo ; the thoughts which most
readily appealed to him concerned the ancestral

splendors of the Dorian race, the deeds of the
Heracleidae, the glories of the heroes from whom
they sprang, the laws and usages which Dorian
tradition had consecrated, the praise of the gods
who protected Dorians and received their worship.
The form of lyric poetry required for the expression of such thoughts was one in which many
performers could take part ; one which should be
impressive on occasions of public solemnity, and
which should satisfy not only ear and mind, but
also that sense of rhythmic movement which had
been developed in Sparta by the habit of gymnas-
tic exercises. Such exercises were not confined
to Spartan men, but were prescribed for Spartan
maidens also ; whose choral dances, moreover,
formed a prominent feature of Spartan festivals.

The first recorded poet of the choral lyric appears at Sparta about the middle of the seventh
century B. C. This is Alcman, a Lydian
who had been brought from Asia Minor   Alcman.
to Sparta as a slave. Such rudimentary choral
poetry as already existed at Sparta had two main
characteristics : it belonged to religious liturgies,
and the words were subordinate to the music.
The solemn νόμοι, "nomes," sung to the gods, and
especially to Apollo, exemplified these traits. The
most general change made by Alcman was in the
direction of secularizing choral poetry. His best
known compositions were odes to be sung by choruses of Spartan maidens, *parthenia*. Into these
he introduced a large variety of feelings and inter-

ests which had no connection with religious ritual.
The sentiments were sometimes those of the poet
himself, sometimes those of the maidens by whom
the ode was sung.   Occasionally there was a kind
of lyric dialogue between the poet and his chorus.
These *parthenia* were composed in strophe and
antistrophe, and were accompanied by the flute.
One of the most notable fragments, in which the
poet distinguishes and compliments individual
maidens of the chorus by name, was found in
Egypt in 1855.   In another fragment, consisting
of four hexameters, Alcman bewails that he is
now too infirm to move round swiftly with the
dancers ; he wishes that he were like the sea-bird
called "cerylus," "that sea-blue bird of spring,"
who skims the bright surface of the waves with
the halcyons.   He also composed hymns to the
gods, and to the Spartan demigods Castor and
Pollux ; choral songs, too, for men and boys at
the festival called *Gymnopaedia*, and marching-
songs for the Spartan troops.   A portion of his
poetry, however, seems to have had no link with
any public occasion, and to have been merely the
expression of his own feelings.   His sympathy
with external nature was evidently true and keen.
We have his description of a serene night in Lace-
daemon, as he saw it in that fair valley of the Eu-
rotas, under the grand cliffs of Taÿgetus : "The
summits of the mountains are sleeping, and the
ravines, the headlands, and the torrent courses, the
leaves that the black earth nourishes, and all creep-

ing things, the wild creatures of the hills, and the race of bees, and the monsters in the depths of the dark sea ; and sleep is upon the tribes of wide-winged birds." Altogether, the Lydian Alcman is an interesting figure in that age of Sparta, when its stern military life was tempered by a larger measure of liberal culture than in later days. He had the ease and grace of an Ionian, with something of an Asiatic bent towards luxury. Yet his choral poetry must have been in unison with the tastes of his audience. The Spartans for whom he sang were capable of appreciating the blended charms of lyric verse, music, and dance.

Stesichorus of Himera in Sicily (610 B. C.) is a poet of greater importance than Alcman, and must be regarded as the chief repre- Stesichorus. sentative of the Dorian choral lyric in its earlier period ; he is, indeed, the poetical ancestor of Simonides and Pindar. In Alcman, as we have seen, there was a subjective element ; the poet's own feelings found large expression. The choral poetry of Stesichorus, on the other hand, was of a thoroughly objective character, and its peculiar stamp depended on its relation to epos. He composed hymns for those national festivals of Sicily and Magna Graecia in which the heroes were especially honored. These hymns seem to have embraced the whole circle of epic tradition. Heracles, Orestes, the Atreidae, Odysseus, Helen, were among his themes. This was an innovation in the treatment of the hymn, which had hitherto been

addressed to divine persons only.   Alcman had indeed written hymns to Castor and Pollux, but they
were at least demigods, raised above the heroes of
human origin.   Further, the style of Stesichorus
was essentially epic ; the poet's personality appeared
as little as it does in the Homeric poems ; and he
used an artificial epic dialect, with only a slight
tinge of Dorian.   He added an epode to the strophe
and antistrophe ; an improvement commemorated
by a proverbial phrase, "the triad of Stesichorus."
This enlargement of the choral structure suited
his epic subjects, which required a grand and
massive framework.   His choral epic hymns gave
the first hint of the model on which Pindar's magnificent odes of victory are constructed.   He was
a precursor of Pindar also in the bold coinage of
new compound words.   Epic grandeur, in a splendid and spacious choral form, was his charm for
the ancient world.   Simonides couples him with
Homer ; Alexander the Great described him as
a poet worthy to be read by kings ; Quintilian
observes that he sustained the burden of epos
with the lyre.   It should be added that he also
broke new ground in two other fields.   His lyric
treatment of popular love-stories, as in his Rhadina
and Calyca, was the germ of romance, afterwards
developed in prose by the Greek novel-writers.
And his lyric pastoral, Daphnis, was the earliest
example of bucolic poetry.

After Stesichorus, the next considerable name
is that of Ibycus, who flourished about 550 B. C.

The place held by Ibycus is in one respect unique. He is the only poet in whom the two great branches of the Greek lyric con- Ibycus. verge, while they still remain distinct. His po- etical life had two periods. In the first he lived at his native Rhegium in southernmost Italy, and wrote choral lyrics in the epic style of Stesichorus. The legend of the Argonauts and stories from the Trojan cycle were handled by him. During the second period of his career he lived in the Ionian island of Samos, at the court of the tyrant Poly- crates ; and here he composed love-poetry, which, to judge by the fragments, was more Aeolian in its passion than anything written since the days of Sappho. It recalls Sappho in this, also, that the portrayal of passion is joined to a vivid feeling for the beauties of nature. Thus Ibycus says : " In spring the Cydonian apple-trees put forth blossoms, watered by the river-streams where the Nymphs have their inviolable haunt ; and the vine-buds come forth, growing under the foliage of the vine-shoots. But for me Love knows no season of slumber, — like the north wind of Thrace, that rages amid lightnings." Love comes upon Ibycus, " dark as the storm, a stranger to fear ; " and he trembles at the god's approach. Similarly, Sappho compares the Love-god to a mountain whirlwind uprooting oaks. The Eros of these poets is a fierce and dreadful power ; not the play- ful boy Eros of later poetry. We are reminded of the words in which Dante describes the apparition

of Love : " There seemed to be in my room a mist
of the color of fire, within which I discerned the
figure of one of terrible aspect." It was by his
later or quasi-Aeolian work, not by his earlier work
on epic themes, that Ibycus was best remembered
in Greek literature.

The last great name before Pindar is that of
Simonides. He was born at Ceos in or
Simonides. about 556 B. C., being some sixteen years
younger than Anacreon, and about thirty-four
years older than Pindar. An Ionian by birth and
by temperament, he chose the Dorian choral form
for his lyrics, which were composed in an artificial dialect like that of Stesichorus, — epic with a
Dorian tinge. As Anacreon is the Ionian of a
luxurious Asiatic type, Simonides is the Ionian
who has felt the chastening and bracing influence
of Athens. He was a poet not only of great gifts,
but also, in some directions, of marked originality.
Stesichorus extended the scope of the choral hymn
from gods to heroes ; Simonides was perhaps the
first who successfully extended it from the heroes
to contemporary men. He wrote odes of victory,
" epinicia," celebrating the successes of competitors
in the great national games, and in these odes probably dwelt more on the details of the particular
victory than Pindar usually does ; also " encomia,"
odes in praise of men notable by position or
achievement, which had less of a public character
than the odes of victory, and were often intended
to be sung at private banquets. One specimen,

which has come down to us nearly entire, is the
" encomium " on the Thessalian tyrant Scopas,
whose guest the poet had been.   The last ten
years of his life were passed with Hieron, the
tyrant of Syracuse, where he is said to have died,
at the age of ninety, in 467 B. C. Such knowledge
as we possess concerning the life and character of
Simonides exhibits him as a clever and versatile
man of the world, with all the subtle and graceful Ionian gifts, but without much depth of conviction or feeling. His pathetic power in poetry
was, indeed, renowned, and in this quality he was
ranked even above Pindar. It was Simonides who
first made the " threnos," or dirge, an accepted
form of lyric poetry. But his pathos was due principally to the perfect purity of style, the unerring
sense of proportion, the exquisite feeling for harmony, with which he knew how to adorn the traditional topics of an epitaph. This fact is illustrated by his verses on the heroes of Thermopylae,
— verses justly celebrated for a beauty of form
which no prose version can even suggest : " Glorious was the fortune of those who died at Thermopylae, and fair is their fate ; their tomb is an
altar.   Others are bewailed, but they are remembered ; others are pitied, but they are praised.
Such a monument shall never moulder, nor shall
it be defaced by all-conquering Time. This sepulchre of brave men has taken the glory of Hellas
to dwell with it ; be Leonidas the witness, Sparta's
king, who has left behind him the great beauty of

prowess and an immortal name." More famous
still is the poet's description of Danaë, with the
infant Perseus, afloat in a chest on the stormy sea,
under the stars ; nothing could be more exquisite
than the contrast between the fierce elements that
rage around and the fair sleeping child, watched
by the young mother, so anxious, so helpless, so
forsaken, apparently, by the divine lover, Zeus,
withdrawn in the recesses of that starry sky, to
whom she makes her timid prayer, — not for herself, but for her child. Simonides was, in his own
sphere, a consummate artist. The slender remains
of his work show few traces of fire or passion,
but they prove an unsurpassed command of all the
graces that can touch and charm.

Kindred though less eminent gifts won renown
for his sister's son, Bacchylides of Ceos, a Bacchylides.
lyric poet who also was numbered among
the foremost nine. The disciple and imitator of
his uncle, Bacchylides was admired especially for
smoothness and finish. Like Simonides, he was a
welcome guest at the court of Hieron, and wrote an
ode of victory on that prince's success in the chariot-race of 472 B. C., the same which is immortalized
in Pindar's first Olympian ; but his home, according
to Plutarch, was in Peloponnesus. The most distinctive branch of his work was probably that in
which he gave a choral treatment to themes of
social pleasure ; and the fragments, scanty though
they are, indicate a vein of genial gaiety which reminds us both of Anacreon and of Horace. His

style is now best represented by some verses which describe the joys of peace with much picturesque detail.   It is an interesting conjecture that the paean in which these verses occurred may have been written at a time when the long struggles with Persia had just been closed by the victories of Cimon.

Reserving Pindar for a separate treatment, I would conclude this sketch of the lyric development by indicating some of the causes why the existence of Greek lyric poetry was not more prolonged.   After the days of Simonides and Pindar it languished, and soon perished.   Why was this so? *Causes which led to the extinction of lyric poetry.*

As to the Aeolian lyric poetry, that had been virtually extinct from a still earlier time.   It could flourish only where the conditions amidst which Sappho and Alcaeus lived were at least partially continued, and where the Aeolian fire burned in spirits like theirs.   Sweetness and light, even when Athenian, were not enough to nourish Aeolian song.   But when the choral lyric had once been transplanted from its Dorian birthplace to Attica, as it was by Simonides and his contemporaries, why should it not have continued to thrive there?   It was well suited to the purposes of Athenian public ritual, and, in the hands of Simonides, had become popular with Athenians.

One cause may be recognized in the diminished number of forms for choral lyrics which Athenian life afforded.   In the seventh century B. C., the

period at which the intellectual culture of Sparta
reached its highest level, the lyrists whom Sparta
attracted and honored found one of their best
opportunities in those choral dances of Spartan
maidens for which *parthenia* like those of Alcman were composed.   But the Attic maiden was
brought up in a comparatively strict seclusion ;
the Dorian *parthenia* were wholly opposed to
Attic feeling and usage.   With regard to other
species of the choral lyric, most of them were
eclipsed at Athens by the popularity of one, the
choral hymn to Dionysus, known as the dithyramb.   And the dithyramb in its turn lost much
of its hold upon public favor when a more brilliant
and enthralling form of the Dionysus cult had
been matured in the drama.   Meanwhile, the ode
of victory, so popular in the age of Simonides and
Pindar, gradually died out in the latter part of the
fifth century B. C., as the divisions and troubles of
Hellas began to react upon the national festivals.
And when, in the time of the Peloponnesian war,
the dithyramb made a last effort to compete with
drama at Athens, that effort only hastened the
extinction of lyric poetry.   The dithyrambic poets
now sought to please by extravagance ; and the
art of music itself was corrupted by an excess
of florid ornament.   Attic comedy, with its ridi-
cule of these things, well interprets the moribund
phase of lyric poetry.

But that poetry had left imperishable monuments.   We have seen how elegy gave utterance

to patriotic exhortation, to tender sentiment, to political wisdom or philosophic reflection, and to grief for the dead; how
iambic poetry became the weapon of satire, but also, like elegy, a more general vehicle of self-expression, especially in animated argument or self-defence; how the lyric monody gave a voice to Aeolian passion and worship of beauty, a voice more feebly echoed in the voluptuous strains of the Ionian; and how the choral lyric, with its massive melodies, became the organ of Dorian life, civil or religious, of heroic legend, of congratulation to victorious athletes, or of the solemn dirge for the departed. In each and all of these kinds, the sure instinct of the Greeks had created a harmony between form and subject, a harmony infinitely varied, but always satisfying the demands of an artistic sense. Such a survey, though rapid, will have prepared us to appreciate the poet in whom the lyric development culminates.

V

In the almost total loss of Greek lyric poetry
the modern world has one consolation : the poet
who closed the series of the masters was ac-
counted the greatest of all.   Sappho might be unapproachable in her kind ; Stesichorus and Simonides might be preëminent in certain qualities
respectively ; but in range of power and loftiness
of inspiration there was no rival to Pindar.   This
was the general and settled verdict of antiquity,
in days when all the materials for a comparison
existed.   And though we possess only one class
of Pindar's compositions, the class is that by
which he had gained his widest popularity.   If
the Alexandrian critics had been asked to name
any one kind of poem as characteristic of him, it
is probable that they would have chosen the odes
of victory, and there can be little doubt that the
majority of ancient readers would have confirmed
their choice.   In relation to the development of
Greek poetry, Pindar has a twofold interest: he
continues the tradition which begins with Alcman
and Stesichorus, while at the same time he may
be regarded as, in a certain sense, the precursor
of the Attic drama.

Little is known concerning his life.   He was

born near Thebes in 522 B. C., being thus a contemporary of Aeschylus, and survived the _{Life of} year 452 B. C.; the date of his death is _{Pindar.} unknown. He enjoyed an elaborate and many-sided training in the complex art of choral lyric composition. He belonged to one of the noblest families in Greece, that of the Aegeidae, _{His family.} which had branches at Thebes, Sparta, and Cyrene; and he stood in an intimate relation with the priesthood of Apollo at _{His relation} Delphi. These facts are of cardinal _{to Delphi.} importance for a comprehension of his poetry. In his whole view of life he is an Hellenic aristocrat, profoundly convinced that men who trace their lineage to a hero have a strain of divine blood, which gives them natural advantages, moral and intellectual no less than physical, over other men. And he has also a priestly tone; he is an expounder of religious and ethical precepts, who can speak in the lofty and commanding accents of Delphi.

The forty-four odes of victory (*epinikia*) represent a type of poem which Pindar had _{The ode of} received from predecessors. Archilo- _{victory.} chus had written a song to Heracles and Iolaus, with the refrain τήνελλα καλλίνικε ("See, the conquering hero comes"), which had long been in use at Olympia, and was still popular in Pindar's time. In the course of the sixth century B. C., which saw a great development of the Greek national games, the more elaborate " ode of victory " came into being. Simonides, thirty-four years older than Pindar, was the first composer whose odes of victory became celebrated.

The first difficulty for moderns, when they try to appreciate the work achieved by Pindar in this field, is that of conceiving the ancient festivals themselves which called forth these odes. What was the meaning of a victory in the games at Olympia, Delphi, Nemea, or the Isthmus? What kind of feelings did it evoke? Perhaps it would be hardly possible for us moderns to imagine these things adequately, even if we knew more than we do. The best resource is to make certain leading points clear to ourselves, and then combine them, as well as we can, in a mental picture.

The Olympian festival. Taking the Olympian festival, then, as the greatest, we may say, first of all, that the spectacle was one of extraordinary brilliancy. The "altis," or sacred precinct, of Olympia, richly adorned with the most splendid works of art, was a focus of Panhellenic religion. In the midst of it was the ancient altar of Zeus, representing the earliest Hellenic phase of the sanctuary, when the worship of Zeus was combined with the cult of the hero Pelops. This was the altar at which the Iamidae, the hereditary soothsayers, practised their rites of divination by fire, in virtue of which Olympia is saluted by Pindar as "mistress of truth." A little to the west of this was the Pelopion, a small precinct in which sacrifices had been offered to Pelops from the time when

Achaeans founded Pisa. South of the Pelopion stood the temple of Zeus. The easternmost portion of this temple was open to the public; the middle portion was probably the place where the wreaths were presented to the victors; the westernmost contained the image of Olympian Zeus, forty feet high, wrought in ivory and gold by Pheidias, and inspired by these words of Homer: "The son of Cronus spake, and nodded his dark brow, and the ambrosial locks waved from the king's immortal head, and he shook great Olympus." Externally this temple was richly adorned with sculpture. The east front exhibited twenty-one colossal figures by Paeonius, a group representing the moment before the chariot-race between Oenomaus and Pelops. The west front showed the fight of the Lapithae and the Centaurs. On the metopes were depicted the twelve labors of Heracles.

Other temples within the altis were those of Hera and the Mother of the Gods. There was also a large number of votive edifices, including the twelve treasure-houses, having the character of small Doric temples, erected by twelve Greek states in honor of the Olympian Zeus. Olympia was not merely a sanctuary, but also the political centre of a league, — a sacred city; and therefore the sacred precinct included a town hall and an agora, while outside of it were a council hall, a gymnasium, and other buildings.

On the east of the altis was the stadion, an ob-

long enclosure used for the foot-races, as well as for
the contests in boxing, wrestling, leaping, quoit-
throwing, and javelin-throwing. It is computed
that upwards of 40,000 spectators could have seen
these contests from the neighboring slopes. The
hippodrome, for chariot-races and horse-races, extended south and south-east of the stadion. The
valley of the Alpheus is itself of great beauty.
Looking eastward, one sees the snow-crowned
ranges of Erymanthus and Cyllene in Arcadia.
Imagine what it must have been when all those
treasures of art, from which the Hermes of Prax-
iteles and the winged Victory of Paeonius are
mere waifs and strays, were seen in the warm
sunlight of September! One can understand the
orator Lysias calling Olympia the "fairest place
in Greece." At this festival, all parts of Hellas
— from the furthest settlement in the western
Mediterranean to the colonies of Asia Minor, the
Euxine, or Libya — were represented by their
foremost men, — the foremost in athletic prowess,
the foremost in poetry, music, eloquence, the
foremost in wealth and power. To enter for the
chariot-race was a costly ambition : a rich man
who did so was considered as reflecting honor on
his city ; and a Sicilian prince such as Hieron or
Theron welcomed the opportunity, not only for
the sake of displaying his resources, but also as a
means to popularity.

Finally, the whole festival was profoundly penetrated by religious feeling, which gave it solemnity

without overclouding its free joyousness. The
gods, Zeus above all, and the heroes, especially
Heracles and Pelops, were present amidst their
worshipers, glorious in the creations of art, and
were felt as watching, inspiring, and rewarding
the competitors. There is therefore nothing in
modern life that can properly be compared with
a victory at Olympia. The modern horse-race or
boat-race may attract vast crowds, and may even
assume the importance of a public holiday ; but
the Olympian gathering was not merely that : it
was also a religious celebration. There is a still
further difference. The glory of the modern race-
winner or athlete is brief ; it lives in the memory
of a few, but not with the public. The Olympian
victor, however, was a distinguished man from
that moment to the end of his days. He had shed
lustre on his native city, and was sure of such
honors as it could bestow. His name was recorded
at Olympia. Go where he might throughout
Hellas, the title which he had won (ὀλυμπιονίκης)
sufficed to procure him a more than respectful
welcome. This permanent renown had its coun-
terpart in the permanent value attached to odes of
victory like Pindar's. Such an ode was indeed an
occasional poem, in the sense that it was written
to celebrate a particular event ; but it was not
ephemeral. An *epinikion* by Pindar was an abiding monument, an heirloom for the victor, his
family, and his city. Thus the ode in which Pindar celebrated the victory of the Rhodian Diagoras

is said to have been copied in letters of gold, and deposited in the temple of Athena at Lindus in Rhodes. The anxiety of the foremost men in Hellas to obtain such a memorial can easily be understood, even though they may not have believed the poet's true prophecy, that his tribute, besides travelling further, would live longer than the marble of the sculptor.

An ode of Pindar is composed of various elements which are nowhere else so blended Characteristics of Pindar's poetry. in literature, and which in the actual life of Hellas were nowhere so vividly brought together as at Olympia. First of these elements is splendor, — a reflex in Pindar's opulent and brilliant language of the material splendor which Olympia could show in so many forms, — the marble of temples and statues, the brilliant colors which everywhere met the eye when embassies from the courts of Greek princes in Africa or Sicily were present in the altis, and when every city in Hellas that appeared at all was anxious to add something of magnificence to the scene; the splendor of athletic beauty in men and youths, perfectly developed by long months of training; the splendor of rushing movement when chariots swept round the hippodrome, and when speed of foot or disciplined strength was tested in the stadion; the splendor of choral music, and of stately ritual at the altars; the splendor of nature around and above, whether sunshine was lighting up the altis and shining on the

snows of the distant Arcadian hills, or the scene
was steeped in that softer radiance of which Pindar speaks, when "the full orb of the midmonth
moon" looked down at evening on feast and music
and song. As an instance of this quality in Pindar's style, we might take the first words of his
first Olympian : "Water is best, and gold is the
shining crown of lordly wealth, like a flaming fire
in the darkness ; but if thou wouldst sing of prizes
in the games, look not by day for a star in the
lonely heaven that shall rival the gladdening radiance of the sun ; nor let us think to praise a place
of festival more glorious than Olympia." In this
splendor is included swiftness. The frequent and
rapid transition from image to image, from one
thought to another which has started up in the
poet's mind, is one of the reasons why it is impossible truly to represent Pindar in continuous translation.

The second element which Olympia offered to
the sight and the thought, as Pindar
offers it to the thought and the ear, is <small>Linking of present with past.</small>
the kinship of the present with the
heroic past. The sacred ground of Olympia on
which the competitors moved everywhere reminded
them of the heroes, the ancestors of the noblest
Hellenes, the common glory of the Hellenic race.
Here was a memorial of Pelops, there of Heracles,
of Telamon or his son Ajax, of Peleus or his son
Achilles, and many more, — all exemplars of strenuous effort, and of immortal fame won through

effort, by the grace of the gods, and of the poets
whom the gods inspired. Stesichorus had set the
first great pattern of heroic legend treated in lyric
verse. Simonides seems to have dwelt more, in
his odes of victory, on the particular circumstances
of the victory which he was celebrating ; and this
is what might have been anticipated from his general bent. Pindar passes, as a rule, lightly and
briefly over the details of the victory itself, and
then links on his theme to some heroic legend,
which often occupies the bulk of the ode. Towards the end, he returns again to his immediate
theme. In finding a suitable link between theme
and myth he shows marvellous skill : it is one of
those points in which his versatile art well repays
close study. But here I would rather draw attention to a larger aspect of his dealing with the heroic legends. These legends serve to invest the
particular victory with a general significance, and
to raise our thoughts from the latest victor towards
one who strove and prevailed in far-off days. They
lend an ideal charm to a triumph of which the
interest would otherwise be mainly local or personal ; and in doing this they render Pindar's poetry once more a faithful mirror of Olympia. The
youngest conqueror who had just received his chap-
let of wild olive moved in an atmosphere of memories which raised his achievement to a still higher
level by connecting it with the ancestral glories
of his race.

A third element common to the Olympian altis

and the Pindaric ode is counsel. When the priests
sprung from Iamus stood beside the altar of Zeus, and read the fiery signs, they
expounded to men the omens of the future. The
athlete about to enter the stadion saw before him
an altar of Kairos, personified Opportunity, the
power that enables competitors to seize the critical moment. In such forms, and many others, the
promptings or warnings of divine counsel were
expressed at Olympia ; but this was not all. The
assembled Hellenes might there hear the voice of
philosopher, or poet, or statesman, who chose that
occasion to urge lessons of wisdom. Pindar is
thoroughly in harmony with the genius of the
national festivals when he weaves precepts of religion or ethical maxims into the richly embroi-
dered texture of his odes. He interprets no special
theory ; rather he gives an impressive utterance to
sentiments and rules of conduct which were generally current among Hellenes, — summing up, as
it were, the teaching of Hellenic experience in a
manner appropriate to such a festival. And as
the Iamidae might have spoken from their altar in
the altis, so Pindar speaks from the spiritual van-
tage-ground of his relation with Delphi. That is,
he speaks loftily, with authority ; and not seldom
his phrases have an oracular stamp, being terse,
strangely worded, or even enigmatic.

There is yet one other feature in which the mind
of Pindar reflects Olympia. The festival brought
Greeks together from the whole Hellenic world.

The imagination of Pindar has a corresponding
_{Panhellenic} tendency to range swiftly over the entire
_{range.} area of Hellas, including the remotest
regions to which Hellenes had penetrated. How
spacious a fancy appears in his figurative description of a man whose hospitalities were unstinted
and continual : " Far as to the Phasis was his voyage in summer days, and in winter to the shores
of Nile." When his song has had free course, he
thinks of it as a ship that has sailed westward,
even beyond the gates of the Mediterranean, and
cries, " None may pass beyond Gadeira into the
gloom of the west ; set our sails once more for the
land of Europa." A voyage to the Pillars of Heracles furnishes him with a comparison for the utmost extent of good fortune. Here, as in his lofty
flight and in his swift descent upon his object, he
is indeed the eagle among poets, who surveys the
whole field of Hellenic existence, while his pier-
cing glance darts from land to land and from city
to city.

Such, then, are the principal elements common
to the festival and the poetry : splendor of light
and color, of physical beauty, of swift movement
and strenuous effort, of choral music and stately
worship, of natural scenery ; vivid sympathy between the present and the heroic past ; wisdom
speaking by the voice of priest and prophet ; a
feeling for the unity of Hellas, quickened by the
sense of its vastness and variety.

The choral form in which Pindar has blended

these elements, and the manner of blending them, are more difficult to describe. The first Olympian ode may be taken as typical. The ode, of one hundred and sixteen Analysis of the first Olympian. verses, is composed in four triads of twenty-nine verses each ; the triad consisting of a strophe and antistrophe, each of eleven verses, followed by an epode, of seven verses. The chorus, in singing each strophe and antistrophe, accompanied their song with rhythmic dancing ; in singing each epode they remained stationary. This ode was in honor of a victory in the horse-race at Olympia, won by Hieron, the ruler of Syracuse, in 472 B. C., and was intended for performance at Hieron's court. It begins with this immediate theme, Hieron's victory ; then passes to the legend of Tantalus and his son Pelops ; and ends with a further reference to Hieron. These three sections, beginning, middle, and end, do not correspond precisely with the limits of triads ; but we may say, roughly, that the first triad is given to Hieron, the second and third triads are given to the myth, and the last triad returns to the subject of the first.

The sequence of thought is as follows : Olympia is the most splendid of festivals, peerless as the sun in the heavens. The victory of Hieron at Olympia has given him fame in the land of Pelops ; *whom* the mighty sea-god Poseidon loved. That relative pronoun " whom," which comes in so naturally, is the link between theme and myth. " Pelops, whom Poseidon loved, from the moment

when Pelops was born with his ivory shoulder."
Now, the ordinary legend did not say that Pelops
was born with an ivory shoulder : it told how the
Lydian king Tantalus, when the gods honored him
by coming as guests to his table, slew his son
Pelops, and set the flesh before them ; the goddess
Demeter unwittingly ate of the shoulder ; then
the gods ordered Hermes to put the remains into
a caldron, from which Pelops came out miracu-
lously re-created, but without this shoulder ; and
Demeter supplied its place by a shoulder of ivory.
Pindar rejects this version, because it dishonors
the immortals (that is, makes Demeter a cannibal), and tells the story thus : The sea-god Poseidon carried the young Pelops off from the banquet
to Olympus, and then the spiteful neighbors of
Tantalus invented the cannibal feast to explain
the boy's disappearance. Tantalus was doomed to
his fearful punishment in the lower world, not for
serving up his son to the gods, but for stealing
their nectar and ambrosia, and giving them to his
mortal companions. And therefore the gods would
not allow his son to remain in Olympus. They
sent Pelops back, " to be numbered once more with
the short-lived race of men." As the youth grew to
manhood he fell in love with Hippodameia, daughter of Oenomaus, king of Elis. Her hand could
be won only by defeating her father in the chariot-
race ; and death was to be the penalty of failure.
The young Pelops went and stood on the seashore
in the night, and called aloud on the sea-god who

had once borne him to Olympus. Poseidon appeared to him; Pelops told his wish, and prayed for the god's help in the contest with Oenomaus, full, as he well knew, of dire peril. " But, seeing that men must die, wherefore should a man sit idly in obscurity, nursing a nameless old age? No!" he cries, " this struggle shall be my task, and do thou give the issue that I desire." Then Poseidon gave him a golden chariot, and horses, winged, untiring. Pelops overcame Oenomaus, and won Hippodameia. And now the grave of Pelops is honored beside the stream of the Alpheus, and his glory is bound up with that of Olympia, " *where* speed and strength are tried."

The myth is finished; and another link like that which knitted proem with myth has been forged to knit myth with conclusion : " Olympia, where speed and strength are tried. He who conquers there hath delicious sunshine in his life henceforth, so far as the games can give it." And as the future is hidden from men, sufficient unto the day is the good thereof. The victory of Hieron claims this Aeolian song; and if the god should not forsake him, he will receive such a tribute again. Greatness has many forms and levels ; may Hieron hold throughout life his supreme power, and the poet his supreme renown.

With this haughty parallel between Hieron and himself, as to degree of eminence in their respective ways, Pindar characteristically closes the first Olympian ode. The outline just given will serve

to show the nature of the framework, the character of the transitions, the manner in which a moralizing strain is mingled with the others. As to
the effect which such an ode would have
General effect of a Pindaric ode. produced when performed with choral
music and dance, the nearest modern
analogy — distant though it be — must be sought
in the sphere of music rather than in that of
poetry. Oratorios such as the Messiah or Israel
in Egypt are at least nearer to Pindar, in their
manner of affecting the hearers, than any kind
of modern literature. There is, of course, a difference which at once limits even this imperfect
analogy, namely, that in Pindar's poetry, as in
all Greek lyrics of the best age, the words were
paramount, and the music subordinate. But the
comparison between the Pindaric ode and the ora-
torio, so far as it is valid at all, does not depend
on the relation between words and music. It
turns rather on those rapid transitions from one
tone of feeling to another, from storm to calm,
from splendid energy to tranquillity, from trium-
phant joy to reflection or even to sadness, which in
Pindar are so frequent and so rapid that they are
reconciled with art only by the massive harmonies
of rhythm and language which hold them together ; harmonies for which two conditions were
indispensable, — a language with the unrivalled
qualities of the Greek, and .an artist supremely
distinguished by rhythmical and musical power
over words. No Greek except Pindar succeeded

in making such harmonies; Pindar himself could
hardly have made them in any modern tongue.
For in the higher poetry, especially when it employs the grand style, the movement of every
modern language is slower than that of Greek.
But modern music allows of transitions from
mood to mood as varied and almost as rapid as
Pindar's; and here again it is the framework of
harmony which makes them possible.

It has been the tendency of much criticism,
both ancient and modern, to convey the Pindar as an
impression that Pindar's genius is of artist.
that impetuous kind which scorns all restraints of
traditional rule, rushes onward without premedi-
tation or pause, and wins its triumphs by the
sheer vehemence of masterful inspiration. Horace has done much to diffuse this conception of
the Theban poet by comparing him to the mountain stream, swollen with rains, which has over-
flowed its banks, and rushes downward in a thun-
derous torrent. In modern times, it was not until
Boeckh and Dissen had brought order out of the
apparent chaos of his metres that this notion of
his lawlessness began to be dissipated. Every
one of his odes is, in fact, a work of the most
elaborate and complex art, calculated and refined
to the smallest detail. It is enough to mention
three things out of several which demanded the
artist's thought and tact.

First, as the compass of the ode is usually
moderate, — the fourth Pythian being the only

one which exceeds five triads, — he had to plan a
symmetrical distribution of his material, so that
proem, central part, and ending should be rightly
proportioned to each other.   And if, as was usually the case, some heroic myth was to be introduced, he had to consider the links with such
myths which could be furnished by the family of
the victor, or by the victor's city, or by some circumstance of the victory itself.   Secondly, he had
to decide the musical mode to which the poem
was to be set.   The Dorian mode breathed a
grave, earnest, manly spirit; the Aeolian was more
joyous and animated, with the tone of . brilliant
and chivalrous festivity; the Lydian, which Pindar uses more rarely, had a tender and pensive
character suited to dirges.   Each style of music
had certain metres which were specially congenial
to it.   Thirdly, the choice of musical mode and
of metre affected the complexion of the dialect.
Pindar's dialect is, in its basis, the same as that
which Stesichorus adopted when he set the first
example of treating heroic themes in lyric form.
It is the epic, a variety shaped by poetical artists,
and not corresponding exactly with any spoken
idiom.   But Pindar tempers this with Dorisms, or
Aeolisms,—Asiatic rather than Boeotian Aeolisms,
— in varying proportions, according to the musical
style and the metre in which he is writing.

These three points suffice to show that Pindar,
in composing an *epinikion*, was an artist working
under manifold demands on observance of rule and

tradition. The most careful thought, the nicest care, were required at every step. Stress must be laid upon this aspect of his work, because it is apt to be overlooked. But there is, of course, another aspect also. The torrent is not a good simile, but the boldness of Pindar's ori- His bold ginal genius is evident. The only rea- originality. son which moderns could find for doubting it is that he so often asserts it. It must be remembered, however, that Pindar is the inspired poet, who feels, as a Greek of his age would feel, that his gift is strictly divine, — that Apollo or the Muse is speaking through his lips, — and that to exalt his own gift is to honor the divinity who bestows it. Certainly it cannot have been altogether pleasant to be a minor poet in Pindar's time : he tells these struggling contemporaries, with a sublime candor, that he is the eagle, while they are ravens and daws. The impression given by Pindar's style is that he is borne onward by the breath of an irresistible power within him, eager to find ample utterance, immense in resources of imagery and expression, sustained on untiring wings. After the longest and highest flight he always seems to have strength in reserve ; after the largest manifestations of his opulent fancy we can feel that there is inexhaustible wealth behind. It is the union of this mighty spirit and this magnificent abundance with the Greek artist's disciplined instinct of self-control and symmetry that renders Pindar unique.

Particular notice is due to the stamp of his diction. Other great poets have been dis-

Pindaric
diction.

tinguished by more delicate felicity, more
chastened beauty of phrase, more faultless and
unimpeachable taste. Sappho and Simonides, to
take only lyric examples, exhibit even in the few
fragments that remain certain charms of this kind
which Pindar lacks; but there is one gift in which
he is absolutely alone. It is one which could
find full scope only within the grand framework of the Dorian choral lyric, — the faculty of
shaping magnificent phrases, and giving them exactly their right setting in the spacious verse, so
that they at once delight the ear and charm the
imagination. Consider, for instance, the line describing how Jason, protected by Medea's spells,
was able to harness the fire-breathing bulls : —

εἶχετ᾽ ἔργου· πῦρ δέ νιν οὐκ ἐόλει παμφαρμάκου ξεινᾶς ἐφετμαῖς.

Who but Pindar could have put the last three
words together? In these carven marble blocks
of language we often find some stately epithet,
perhaps fashioned by the poet himself, as, ἀστέων
ῥίζαν φυτεύσεσθαι μελησίμβροτον. But even the com-
monest words can be thus moulded by him into
forms which haunt the memory, as when Medea
says, referring to the piece of Libyan earth that
was lost overboard from the Argo : —

ἐναλίαν βᾶμεν σὺν ἅλμᾳ
ἑσπέρας, ὑγρῷ πελάγει σπομέναν.

It is in some of these phrases, where Pindar has

used long compound words, that he has more especially given occasion for the charge of bombast.
Voltaire called him "this inflated Theban," and
said that Pindar's French translator, M. de Chau-
mont, had endowed the turgid Greek with such
clearness and beauty as he could claim. Mr. Matthew Arnold describes Pindar as "the poet on
whom, above all other poets, the power of style
seems to have exercised an inspiring and intoxicat-
ing effect," — which implies at least a certain absence of due self-restraint. Few would contend
that Pindar's marvellous wealth of ideas and words
never betrayed him into excess. One remembers
what Ben Jonson said of Shakespeare : " He was
indeed honest, and of an open and free nature,
had an excellent fancy, brave notions, and gentle
expressions ; wherein he flowed with that facility
that sometimes it was necessary he should be
stopped." Yet one would have been sorry, on the
whole, to have had Shakespeare regulated by Ben
Jonson ; and surely we may be glad that Pindar
was not governed by a modern standard of lyric
sobriety. But what I wish to point out here is the
intimate relation between the rhythmical structure
of Pindar's odes and that moulding of phrases in
which he is a very Michael Angelo of language.
Learn a few strophes of the fourth Pythian by
heart, carefully studying the metre at the same
time, and then you will apprehend, more clearly
than before, two things, — the plastic power over
words which Pindar wields, and the extent to

which even those phrases which modern criticism might deem somewhat turgid — ποικιλοφόρμιγγος ἀοιδᾶς, for instance — are excused by the fact that they harmonize with the genius of these spacious measures which sustain the majestic structure of the Dorian ode. If we could hear such an ode performed with the music to which it was wedded by Pindar, this relation would undoubtedly be still more apparent.

The power of poetry is inseparable, in Pindar's thought, from the power of music, and both are symbolized by the lyre, — "joint possession," as he calls it, "of Apollo and the Muses." "O golden lyre, joint possession of Apollo and the dark-haired Muses, thou at whose bidding the dancer's step begins the festal dance, thou whose signs the singers obey, when thy quivering notes raise the prelude of the choral song! Thou canst quench even the thunderbolt, whose spear is of perennial fire ; and the eagle, king of birds, slumbers on the sceptre of Zeus, suffering his swift wings to droop at his sides ; for thou hast sent a mist of darkness on his arched head, a gentle seal upon his eyes, and he heaves his back with the rippling breath of sleep, spellbound by thy trembling strains. Yea, the violent god of war forgets the cruel sharpness of his spears, and yields his melting soul to slumber ; for thy shafts subdue the minds of the immortals, by virtue of the art which is from Leto's son and the deep-bosomed Muses.

His feeling for the power of music. Invocation of the lyre (Pyth. i.).

" But all creatures that Zeus loves not are dis-
mayed when they hear the music of the Pierides,
whether on land or on the raging deep ; as that
foe of the gods who lies in fearful Tartarus, Typhon
of the hundred heads, reared of old in the famed
Cilician cave. But now Sicily and the sea-restrain-
ing cliffs above Cumae press down his shaggy
breast, and a pillar of heaven holds him fast, even
hoary Aetna, nurse of keen snow through all the
year ; whose secret depths hurl upward pure foun-
tains of unapproachable fire ; in the daytime, those
rivers pour forth a stream of lurid smoke, but in
the darkness a red rolling flame sweeps rocks with
a roar to the wide deep."

We observe here Pindar's feeling for what is
grand or terrible in nature, one which His sense of
elsewhere finds only limited expression grandeur or
beauty in
in Greek poetry of this age. Thus Aes- nature.
chylus, who also speaks of Aetna in eruption, em-
phasizes rather its destructive effect on human
labor : "Rivers of fire shall break forth, rend-
ing with fierce fangs the level meads of fruitful
Sicily." Nor is Pindar less in sympathy with gentler aspects of natural beauty. In the fragment
of a dithyramb he speaks of the season " when
the chamber of the Hours is opened, and nectar-
breathing plants perceive the fragrant spring.
Then are the lovely tufts of violets strewn over
the divine earth ; then are roses twined in the
hair, and voices of songs sound to the flute, and
choruses chant of bright-wreathed Semele."

Those verses may remind us of the goddesses who were often·represented as young maidens decking themselves with vernal flowers, — the Charites, or Graces. They are the deities who give all things that can rejoice or refine the human spirit, who lend a crowning charm to victory and festivity, who throw a gentle radiance over every form of art, and who are therefore also goddesses of song, especially of such song as Pindar's. His tribute to the power of music should be associated The Charites with his invocation of the Charites : " Il-
(Olymp. xiv.). lustrious queens of bright Orchomenus, who watch over the old Minyan folk, hear me, ye Graces, when I pray ! For by your help come all things glad and sweet to mortals, whether wisdom is given to any man, or beauty, or renown. Yea, the gods ordain not dance or feast apart from the majesty of the Graces. The Graces control all things wrought in heaven ; they have set their throne beside Pythian Apollo of the golden bow ; they adore the everlasting godhead of the Olympian father."

Pindar is never more truly Hellenic than when His views of he mingles his celebration of human
human life. glory with reminders as to the limit of human destiny. The athlete who has won victory by painful self-discipline, the prince whose victory is an illustration of "wealth set off by virtues," like gold set with gems more precious still, have won a noble reward, a very light of life, which burns most brightly when the poet has given

them enduring renown. But they, too, must remember Nemesis. "No mortal can find a path,
by sea or land, to the Hyperboreans: no mortal
can climb the brazen sky." " Let a man remember that his raiment is worn on mortal limbs, and
that the earth shall be his vesture at the last."
"Forecasts of the future are doomed to blind-
ness." " The hopes of men are tossed up and
down, as they cleave the waves of disappoint-
ment." Such sentiments do not, however, cast
any prevailing shadow over Pindar's poetry.
They serve rather to limit the human horizon,
without discouraging effort, or veiling the sunshine which requites it. Definite as are the
bounds of man's lot, he still, as Pindar says, "has
some likeness to the immortals, perchance in
lofty mind, perchance in form." Pindar has
summed up his view in these words: "Things of
a day ! what are we ? what are we not ? Man is a
shadow, a dream. But when the glory of victory
has come, the gift of heaven, then a clear light
rests on men, and their life is serene."

Simonides, in his dirges, seems to have dwelt
chiefly on the pathos of death ; Pindar, in the most
famous fragment of this class, pictures the bliss of
the life in Elysium: "The strength of
the sun shines for them in that world, Elysium.
while it is night with us ; the space before their
city, amid crimson-flowered meadows, has shade of
frankincense trees and wealth of golden fruits.
Some of them take their pleasure with horses or

in feats of strength, and some with dice, and some with harps ; all fair-flowering bliss thrives among them, and fragrance streams ever through the lovely land, as they mingle incense manifold on the altars of the gods, with far-seen fire."

The last aspect of Pindar's work which claims our notice is one of the most interesting, — the relation in which he stands to epos on the one side, and to drama on the other. The scanty fragments of Stesichorus, no less than the notices of him by ancient writers, suggest that his treatment of the heroic myths, though lyric in form, was distinctly epic in manner ; that is, it consisted largely of continuous narrative. The most epic of Pindar's odes is the fourth Pythian, where he tells the story of the Argonauts. Of the two hundred and ninety-nine verses in this ode, the actual story of the Argonauts — apart from Medea's prophecy which is prefixed to it — fills about one hundred and eighty verses. If Pindar's method here — where he makes his nearest approach to epos — be compared with the epic, it will be seen that there are two principal differences. First, he brings out particular moments of the story — single scenes or episodes — with a vividness surpassing that of epic narrative. He succeeds in doing so by the terse brilliancy of his style, which is often marvellously picturesque, and by the short pieces of direct speech which serve to dramatize the speakers.

Pindar's relation to epic poetry.

The fourth Pythian.

What could be more graphic, for instance, than
the picture of the youthful Jason when he suddenly appeared in the market-place of Iolcus, wearing the close-fitting dress of a hunter in the Mag-
nesian forests, with a leopard's skin over it, while
his long bright hair streamed down his back? "He
went straight on, and stood in the market-place
when the crowd was fullest, putting his dauntless
spirit to the proof. They knew not who he was;
but one or another of the awe-struck folk was
moved to say, 'Surely this is not Apollo, no, nor
Aphrodite's lord, of the brazen chariot; and 't is
said that the sons of Iphimedeia have their graves
in bright Naxos, even Otus, and thou, bold king
Ephialtes. Yea, and Tityos hath fallen by the
swift arrow of Artemis, sped from her invincible
quiver, that mortals should not long for loves that
are beyond their reach.' Thus the people spake
to one another." How vivid, again, is the picture
of the moment when the ship Argo is about to
sail from Iolcus, with her crew of heroes, and
Jason, at the stern, pours his libation to Zeus,
after the weighing of the anchor! "The chief
took a golden goblet in his hands, and called on
Zeus, whose spear is the lightning, and on the
rushing strength of waves and winds, and on the
nights, and the paths of the deep; and prayed for
kindly days, and friendly fortune of return. Then
a favoring voice of thunder pealed in answer
from the clouds, and bright flashes of lightning
came bursting through them; and the heroes

were comforted, putting faith in the signs of the god."

This, then, is the first distinction of Pindar here, —the force with which he portrays certain moments. The second is the swiftness with which he glides over all those parts of the story which it does not suit him to elaborate. After the description of Jason ploughing with the dread oxen of Aeëtes, and how he was shown the place where the dragon guarded the golden fleece, Pindar thus cuts the story short : "'Tis long for me to tread the well-worn track ; yea, and I know a speedy path ; I have shown the ways of song to many." Then he suddenly apostrophizes Arcesilas, the prince to whom the ode is addressed, and tells, in only four lines, how Jason slew the dragon, won the fleece, and sailed home with Medea and his comrades.

Continuous epic narrative no longer sufficed for Pindar's contemporaries. The men who had lived through the Persian wars, and who took delight in the national games, had a quickened power of imagining strenuous action. The heroes of the past were believed to have mingled with the Greek warriors, and to have aided them in beating back the foe on sea and land. Pindar's age turned to the heroic legends with a desire to seize each particular episode as vividly as possible, and to bring the heroes into a closer relation with its own life. This tendency, of which the fourth Pythian is the greatest example, can be seen in other odes,

also, where Pindar treats, more briefly, some one
situation or incident taken from the legends. Such
is the picture of the nymph Cyrene, the warlike
huntress in the mountain dells of Pindus,
who, in Pindar's words, "loved not the   The nymph Cyrene (Pyth. ix.).
pacings to and fro before the loom." And
once, he says, "as she struggled alone, without
spear, against a fierce lion, far-darting Apollo, lord
of the wide quiver, found her; and straightway
he called Cheiron from his dwelling, and spake
unto him : 'Son of Philyra, come forth from thy
holy cave, and marvel at the spirit of this woman,
and at her great might, — what battle she wages
here with intrepid brow, — a maiden with heart
too high for toil to quell; her soul is shaken by
no tempest of fear. What man begat her? From
what stock was she reft, to dwell in the secret
places of the shadowy hills?'"

Or, again, take the description of Heracles, as
au infant, strangling the serpents which Hera had
sent to destroy him and his brother Iolaus
in their cradle. When the serpents ap-   The infant Heracles (Nem. i.).
pear there is a general panic : Alcmena's
handmaids are distracted ; warriors come rushing
in with swords. But lo! "the boy Heracles lifted
up his head, and began the fight : he seized the two
serpents by their necks in his sure grasp, and, as
he strangled them, time forced the breath out of
their monstrous forms." Then Amphitryon sends
for the seer Teiresias, who prophesies the child's
great future : "how many lawless shapes of vio-

lence he should destroy on land and sea ; how he
should give to death those hatefullest of men who
walk in guile and insolence ;" and how, at last, for
reward of his toils, " he should receive fair Hebè
for his bride, and hold his marriage feast in the
house of Zeus, well pleased with that dwelling-place
divine." The whole picture of this scene around
the cradle is masterly, — the spectators, first terri-
fied, and then full of joyful amazement, and the
calm prescience of the seer. Not less so is that
scene from the later life of Heracles, when he is
the guest of Telamon in Aegina, and prays to his
divine father that the wish of Telamon's
heart may be granted: " Then Heracles
stretched forth to heaven his unconquer-
able hands, and spake thus : ' O father Zeus, if
ever thou hast heard my prayers with willing heart,
I pray thee now, even now, with strong entreaty,
that thou give this man a brave child of Eriboea, —
a son, strong of body, even as this lion's hide that
floats around me, stripped from the beast that I
slew in Nemea of old, first of my labors ; and may
he have a soul to match.' When Heracles had so
spoken, the god sent forth the king of birds, a
mighty eagle, and sweet pleasure thrilled through
the hero, and he spake as a prophet speaks : ' Telamon, thou shalt have the son whom thou desirest ;
and after the name of the bird that has appeared,
call him Ajax : great shall be his might, and he
shall be terrible in the strife of warring hosts.' "

Let us remember that the setting of these pic-

Heracles pre-
dicts the birth
of Ajax
(Isthm. v.)

tures is the ode of victory. No other form of Greek poem was so intimately bound up with the energies of the present ; Pindar's verse throbs with all those pulses of Hellenic life *Affinity of* which were stirred by the great festivals. *Pindar's spirit to that of* When the heroes of the past were intro- *Attic drama.* duced into such an ode ; when they were made, as Pindar makes them, to stand out before the fancy in deed and word, — then the character of the poem itself gave those persons a new meaning. There might be some implied parallelism between the ancient hero and the living victor ; or the association might be limited to the fact that both were celebrated in the same choral ode. But, in either case, the poetical juxtaposition had a two-fold effect. It threw an ideal light around the living victor ; and it also invested the legendary hero with a new reality. The hero was now drawn within the circle of contemporary interests : those who listened to a choral ode of Pindar, with the Olympian victor whom it glorified present to their eyes, gained a more vivid conception of his heroic prototype.

Thus the lyric poetry of Pindar lends a new vitality to the epic tradition. This vivid sympathy with heroic action, stimulated by the struggles of the present, and yet lifted above it, is the same which received its final expression in the Attic drama. Before Pindar's career was closed Aeschylus had passed away ; Sophocles and Euripides were the rising masters of tragedy. It

would be misleading to exaggerate the degree of
kinship between the spirit of their work and that
of Pindar. But, in the sense which has been defined, a true affinity exists. Pindar, the greatest
of the Greek lyrists, — the most wonderful, perhaps, in lofty power, that the lyric poetry of any
age can show, — holds his title to immortality by
the absolute quality of his work ; but for the history of Greek literature he has also the relative
interest of showing the epic heroes under a new
light, — neither that far-off, though clear, light, as
of a fair sunset, which the lay of the minstrel shed
around them in the palace of Alcinous, nor yet
that searching sunshine of noontide which fell
upon them in the theatre of Dionysus.

VI

THE ATTIC DRAMA

WE have seen how the Dorian choral lyric, as handled by Stesichorus and his successors, had clothed the old epic legends in a new form; one which was peculiarly congenial to the widely spread Dorian family, but which was welcomed also by Hellenes to whom the spirit of Ionian epos had been either alien or unsatisfying. It was a particular species of the choral lyric which, in turn, became the parent of the Attic Drama. Origin of Attic Drama. In drama the heroic myths were once more animated with a new life, — different from that which had been given to them in Ionia, different also from the lyric, and yet preserving elements of both. When Aeschylus created Tragedy, he became, for the Athens and the Hellas of his day, truly a second Homer.

Drama sprang from the species of lyric poem called the dithyramb. The dithyramb The dithyramb. is mentioned first by Archilochus, who describes it as the "beautiful song of Dionysus," and boasts that he knows how to raise that song when inspired by wine. It appears, then, that the dithyramb was originally a convivial song, definitely associated with the god Dionysus. It may also be inferred that it was originally sung by

one voice; it belonged to the "monodic" class of
lyrics. The Greeks seem to have received the cult
of Dionysus from Thrace, a region well known to
Archilochus ; and the dithyramb probably came
along with the cult. The etymology of the word
is unknown. It is conjectured that the first sylla-
ble, *di*, represents the root of δῖος, etc. (compare
διπόλια), and that the word "dithyramb" meant a
divine or excellent θύραμβος. The latter word, also
in the form θρίαμβος, occurs as the name of a song
or dance ; but its origin remains uncertain.

A song to the wine-god, sung under his influence, had presumably a wild, impassioned character, and was accompanied with gesticulation. It
would thus have presented a strong contrast to
the tranquil and solemn *nomos*, "nome," chanted
to Apollo, with which the improved music of Terpander was peculiarly associated. Of the two
styles, that which the nome exhibited was the better suited to the Hellenic nature. The dithyramb,
in its original form, would have been less Hellenic
than Oriental. It is not surprising, then, that
while the nome appears at the beginning of the
lyric period, the dithyramb was the last lyric
species which received an artistic development.

Arion.   This development was due to Arion, of
Methymna in Lesbos, who probably belonged to the Lesbian school of citharodes founded
by Terpander. Corinth was the place at which
Arion produced his choral dithyrambs ; he had been
invited to the court of Periander, who was tyrant

of Corinth from about 628 to 585 B. C. A luxurious and pleasure-loving city, Corinth already knew
the worship of Dionysus, and was generally well
disposed towards novelties of an Oriental character. The chorus which sang a dithyramb was
designated in the fifth century as a κύκλιος χορός, a
circular chorus, probably because it moved in
dance round the circular orchestra, in contradistinction to the tragic chorus, drawn up facing the
actors. In the time of Simonides the number of
such a chorus was fifty, and this number may have
dated from Arion. But the work of Arion was not
merely to make the dithyramb choral. His chorus,
we are told, was composed of satyrs. A The satyr
chorus so composed was called a τραγικὸς chorus.
χορός. The word τράγος, "goat," is used by Aeschylus in a fragment of one of his satyr plays as a
synonym for "satyr." Such "goat" or "satyr"
choruses had existed in the Peloponnesus before
Arion's time. At Sicyon, about 600 B. C., they
pertained to a festival in honor of the hero Adrastus ; and Cleisthenes, who was then tyrant of
Sicyon, is said to have transferred them from the
cult of Adrastus to the cult of Dionysus. The
words in which Herodotus relates this (v. 67) imply that, in his belief at least, the satyr chorus had
previously belonged to the cult of Dionysus, and
that Cleisthenes was merely vindicating the right
of the deity to an honor which had been tempo-
rarily alienated from his worship. When Arion
formed his dithyrambic chorus of satyrs, he was

assigning the song of Dionysus to specially appropriate performers, who stood in a recognized relation to that god. And he was also making the
performance something more lively, more characteristic, than an ordinary choral song. Still, there
was nothing as yet properly dramatic in such an
entertainment.

The dithyrambic chorus, performed by satyrs,
came to Athens during the brilliant reign of
Peisistratus, about the middle of the sixth century. At this period the cult of Dionysus had
already gained a strong hold upon Attica. Peisistratus favored a popular and growing taste by
The Great   establishing a new festival of the god,
Dionysia.   more considerable than any which then
existed, — the Great Dionysia, celebrated in the
later spring, towards the end of March. The
dithyrambic chorus was now added to the regular
attractions of this festival.

The next step towards the creation of drama
Thespis.   was that which is associated with the
name of Thespis. At the Great Dio-
nysia of 534 B. C., Thespis, in producing a dithyrambic chorus, came forward as a reciter of verses,
addressing his chorus of satyrs, and doubtless per-
sonating a satyr himself. The iambic verse had
been at home in Attica since Solon's time, and
here was a ready-made vehicle for a lively address,
humorous or satirical. The satirical iambics of
Archilochus and others had furnished models.
The new departure thus combined an Ionian ele-

ment with the Dorian choral lyric; and that combination was enduring. But even then the entertainment fell short of being dramatic. The reciter
of verses who addressed the dithyrambic chorus
could indeed relate action. But action could not
yet be represented as taking place before the eyes
of the spectators.

In the obscure interval between Thespis and
Aeschylus, the most important name is that of
Phrynichus. Two of his best-known ^{Phrynichus.}
pieces were founded upon contemporary
events. One of these pieces dealt with the cap-
ture of Miletus by the Persians at the close of the
Ionian revolt. The other, entitled the Phoenissae,
turned upon the battle of Salamis. In each the
chorus was, of course, the dominant feature; the
catastrophe was related to them by the single
reciter.

Aeschylus, born in or about 525 B. C., is said
to have made his first appearance as a ^{Aeschylus.}
poet about 500 B. C., and to have gained
the first prize at the Dionysia some sixteen years
later, about 484 B. C. The entertainment which
he found existing was such as Thespis had made
it, — a goat-song, or "tragedy," which was still
essentially lyric, and not yet properly dramatic.
Instead of the single reciter, Aeschylus introduced two persons, both, like the single reciter,
detached from the chorus. These two persons
could hold a dialogue, and could represent action.
By this change, Aeschylus altered the whole char-

acter of the lyric tragedy, and created a drama.
The dialogue between the two actors

The founder of Drama.

now became the dominant feature of the
entertainment; the part of the lyric chorus, though
still very important, had now only a diminished
importance.

In reading the Frogs of Aristophanes, written

Testimony of Aristophanes.

fifty years after the death of Aeschylus,
we see his place in Athenian memory.
That comedy is an inestimable document, of which
the historical value is not impaired by the free
play of humor and of fancy; it is nearer, both in
time and in spirit, to the age of Aeschylus, and is
far more instructive than any other document
that we possess.   There we catch an echo of the
sweet lyrics of Phrynichus, — of those "native
wood-notes wild" which he had warbled as if the
birds had taught him, — a music dying away in
the distance of that century's earliest years, —
the lyrics of which elderly men had heard their
fathers speak with delight.   And there, too, rises
before us a living image of the majestic poet who
had come after Phrynichus, the poet who, first of
the Hellenes, had built up a stately diction for
Tragedy, and also invested it with external grandeur; the poet who had described the battle of
Salamis as he had seen it; whose lofty verse had
been inspired by the wish to nourish the minds of
his fellow-citizens with ennobling ideals, to make
them good men and true, worthy of their fathers
and their city; the poet to whom many an Athe-

nian, sick at heart with the decay of patriotism and
with the presage of worse to come, looked back,
amidst regret for the recent loss of Sophocles and
Euripides, as to one who had been not only the
creator of the Attic drama, but also in his own
person an embodiment of that manly and victorious Athens which was forever passing away.

Before turning to the individual characteristics
of the three tragic masters, it may be   Nature of At-
well to touch briefly on the nature of   tic Tragedy.
Attic Tragedy itself, as it was determined in its
essential features by Aeschylus.

The first point which claims notice is the relation of Attic Tragedy to epos. Aeschylus, or some
one who understood him, said that his tragedies
were morsels from Homer's great feast. It was
Aeschylus who decided, once for all, that the
proper and distinctive material of tragedy was to
be found in the heroic legends. The
rule did not preclude an occasional ex-   Its material.
ception, such as the Persae, but it was of general validity, and was maintained as long as Attic
tragedy lasted. And it was not an arbitrary rule.
The heroic world was that in which, for the
Greeks, the deeds and sufferings of humanity
were raised to an ideal nobleness, an ideal pathos. A Greek who desired that his drama
should lift men's minds into that region, — that
it should nobly move and nobly teach them, —
could go to no other fountain-head than Homeric epos. The age of Aeschylus regarded epos

as history.   Later history could also, doubtless,
supply tragic themes.   The fortunes of the last
Lydian king, as Herodotus narrates them, would
have furnished such a theme ; what could be more
tragic than the fate of Croesus, lured towards the
eastern bank of the Halys by a divine voice which
he had not understood, and, in his abasement,
even under the shadow of death, bringing the
lessons of his own destiny home to the mind of
his Persian conqueror?   But, in that picture of
the past which lived before the imagination of the
men who had fought at Salamis, no heroic glory
lit up the period between Homer and themselves.
Such glory played around the captors of Troy, and
a true kinship with those conquerors of Priam was
felt by the conquerors of Xerxes ; but if Attic
Tragedy was not to idealize the heroism which the
contemporaries of Aeschylus had enacted, then it
must go back to the heroism which the traditions
of their ancestors had consecrated.   The limits of
epos — not absolutely of its actual themes, but at
least of its spirit — were the limits of Attic Tragedy ; the essence of that Tragedy was in viewing
the heights of the past from the heights of the
present, so blending them in a single imaginative
view that the heroic past became, in very truth,
the present.

And this brings us to another point which
Its didactic quality — how limited. should be remembered.   Modern criticism, introspective and analytic, has
pondered particular sayings of Aeschy-

lus, Sophocles, Euripides; it has brought these
sayings together, arranged them under heads, di-
gested them into formulas, linked them by ingenious reconciliations, until, for each of the three
dramatists, it has evolved a certain body of philosophy or theosophy. Such efforts have an interest and a value of their own. But the artificial
method involves a danger of representing the
thought of these poets as more systematic than it
really was. When Aeschylus, for instance, took a
subject from the heroic epos, and made it into
a play or a trilogy, his paramount aim was to
present his story in the most effective and vivid
manner, — that which seemed to him most beautiful and most impressive. He was a poet and an
artist moved by the god to give dramatic embodiment to those great forms, — human, but raised
above common humanity, — from whom the Hellenes traced their lineage, and through whom
their lineage ascended to the gods of their race.
Stirred by that great endeavor, he poured forth
the deepest thoughts and feelings which his life
had bred in him; yes, and felt himself called to be
a teacher — to move the minds and nourish the
hearts of his people. But these thoughts and
sentiments, which he uttered as the course of the
drama suggested, do not warrant the assumption
that the poet had a definite and coherent system of
doctrine in his mind. If, for example, Aeschylus
could be examined on his views of the relations
between fate and free will, modern criticism would

possibly find his answers vague and unsatisfactory — far less ingenious, too, than the answers
which moderns have devised on his behalf. As
for the Athenian spectators in the theatre, they
went to see the heroes in bodily presence, and to
hear their living voices; they went to see what
Aeschylus would make Agamemnon do and say.
They looked also to hear wise thoughts from
actors or from chorus, and they welcomed such
wisdom, which worked upon them mainly by deep-
ening beliefs with which they were already im-
bued. Each of the great dramatists colored the
collective experience of Hellenes with his own
views of life, and gave prominence to certain
thoughts of his own ; but, in so far as Attic Tragedy was directly didactic, the larger part of what
it did consisted in clothing received Hellenic maxims with forms of new energy and beauty.

A third point which is of some moment, if
we wish to apprehend the spirit of Attic
Its portraiture
of character. Tragedy, is the general nature of the
character-drawing. It is a familiar observation
that the characters of Attic Tragedy are rather
types than individuals : and this is true in a relative sense ; it is true for *us*, who are accustomed
to a portraiture of character more minute, fuller
of individualizing touches, than any which Attic
Tragedy attempted. Our standard, in dramatic
portraiture, is the Shakespearian ; the Aeschylean
Clytaemnestra might be described as typical
rather than individual, in comparison with Lady

Macbeth; so might the Sophoclean Oedipus, in comparison with Lear. Nevertheless, when we study Clytaemnestra or Oedipus, we feel not only the breadth and vividness of the poetical conception, but also the number of fine touches by which the effect has been aided. In speaking of "types," then, we must guard against seeming to mean that Clytaemnestra was to Aeschylus, or Oedipus to Sophocles, merely the abstract representative of a certain genus. Each of them was, to the creator, a living individual, definitely and vividly conceived; only the ideal aim of Attic Tragedy imposed a certain restraint upon details, when this individual was to be presented in action and speech. Here, once more, it is the relation of Attic Tragedy to epos that gives us the right gauge. Epos was narrative, dealing with a large compass of material. The conditions of such narrative seldom permitted the epic poet to elaborate pictures of character. The most highly individualized persons of Homeric epos are perhaps Zeus and Hera, whose domestic dissensions are favorable to that result; then Achilles and Odysseus; and then perhaps Nausicaa. But these are exceptional; most of the epic characters are hardly more than adumbrated. Attic Tragedy received its persons from epos, with only a few salient traits prescribed, — sometimes scarcely even so much. Within these mere outlines, the characters were, as a rule, created by the Attic dramatists themselves. Each dramatist could use his own discretion; he was not even bound to be consistent with himself; the Creon of the Oedipus Tyrannus is different from the Creon of the Coloneus; so is the Helen of the Helena from that of the Orestes. Still less did one dramatist feel bound by another's conception; witness the Electra of Sophocles and the Electra of Euripides. But when the creative period of Greek poetry was closed; when the literary poets of a later age, Greek or Roman, looked back on the Attic drama as a whole; then it was recognized that the heroic persons had there been delineated once for all. The characters as drawn in Attic Tragedy were for these later writers the standard conceptions. Clytaemnestra, Oedipus, and the rest had received from the Attic dramatist certain attributes which thenceforth adhered to them. Horace reminds us of this in the Ars Poetica; and Seneca's plays practically illustrate Horace. Thus Attic Tragedy became to the later literature nearly what epos had been to Tragedy. Epos had prescribed outlines which Tragedy had filled in, — observing, while it did so, the limitations imposed by the first law of its being, its ideal scope; and these characters became traditional, — without receiving, however, any further development comparable with that which Tragedy had effected.

Remembering these general qualities of Attic Tragedy, we may next consider the particular stamp impressed upon it by each of the great masters. Among the seven

Distinctive traits of the three masters.

extant plays of Aeschylus, the oldest is the Supplices, which has been conjecturally
placed a year or two before the battle of   Aeschylus.
Marathon. Whatever its precise date may be, it
undoubtedly has the interest of showing us the
creator of Tragedy at a comparatively early moment in his career; as the Oresteia, near the end
of his life, shows us the climax of his achievement.
When the work of Aeschylus is viewed in regard
to its form, the first broad characteristic which
claims notice is his treatment of the   His use of
Chorus. In the Supplices, the Chorus   the Chorus.
is the true protagonist. We are reminded of the
time, then recent, before Aeschylus had introduced the second actor, when Tragedy had been
essentially lyric. And in that choral ode of the
Supplices which invokes blessings upon Dorian
Argos, there is a significant reference to Dorian
lyric poetry, as composed, in various kinds, for
public ritual; "May the singers raise holy song
at the altars, and may the chant, wedded to the
harp, be poured from pure lips." The Danaides,
who form the Chorus of the Supplices, were regu-
larly represented as fifty in number; and it is not
improbable that, in this play, the Chorus consisted
of fifty persons, — the number, as we have seen,
of the cyclic or dithyrambic Chorus. The chorus
of only twelve, used in the later plays of Aeschylus, — representing roughly one quarter of the
cyclic Chorus, — may have come in along with the
tetralogy, presumably his invention. In no other

play is the Chorus quite so important as in the
Supplices ; yet in each of the other six, besides
bearing a large part, it has also a real share in
the action.   Thus in the Prometheus the Ocean
Nymphs are not merely the comforters of the
sufferer, who remain with him throughout; at
the end they defy the Olympian threats, and
resolve to share his doom.   The Persian Elders
in the Persae represent the nation smitten at
Salamis, and interpret the effect of the battle
upon Asia.   In the Seven against Thebes the
Theban maidens are so closely interested in the
events that at the end they even divide into two
factions, one siding with Antigone and the other
with Ismene.   The Elders of Mycenae in the
Agamemnon are outspoken opponents of Clytaemnestra and Aegisthus.   In the Choephori the
Chorus of captive maidens assist the vengeance ;
and the Eumenides, in the play called after them,
have a part second only, if second, to that of
Orestes.

As a lyric poet, in his choral odes, Aeschylus
His style in
lyrics.   has a strongly-marked style, which must
be recognized as altogether his own ; the
history of the choral lyric, so far as we know,
shows nothing resembling it as a whole, nor is
there anything like it in the later dramatists.   A
typical example of this style is afforded by the
first two odes in the Agamemnon.   We find there
three principal characteristics.   First, there is an
epic tone, Homeric in its nobleness, and accord-

ant with the hexameter rhythms which are so largely used; Homeric also in the variety and vivacity given to the narrative by short speeches like those of Calchas and Agamemnon. Secondly, the lyric expression is boldly imaginative, in a manner which sometimes recalls Pindar; thus there is a Pindaric rapidity in the succession of images and metaphors. Thirdly, there is an element of reflection, not practically sententious or didactic, as with Pindar, but rather the outcome of a deeply-brooding mind, with a mystic tinge. The lofty language in which these three qualities are blended exhibits varying harmonies between form and matter. At one moment it has the vigorous directness of Homeric narrative. At another it labors with the stress of conflicting thoughts, as in the verses which picture the anguish of Agamemnon. Or solemn emphasis and intense earnestness are expressed by a cumulative weight of phrase, as in the warning of Calchas, —

μίμνει γὰρ φοβερὰ παλίνορτος
οἰκονόμος δολία μνάμων μῆνις τεκνόποινος.

Again, plastic beauty and human pathos are marvellously united in the description of Iphigeneia, about to die at the altar, and in the passage picturing the desolation of Menelaus. It is needless to multiply illustrations from other plays; but we might mention the two odes of benediction — that of the Danaides for Argos and of the Eumenides for Athens — as examples of a gentle

lyric charm : and, as marking the height of sublimity, that ode in which the Eumenides describe
their own nature and office.

As in the lyrics of Tragedy, so also in dialogue,
the style of Aeschylus is distinctive.
He was not, indeed, the first who had
lent dignity and beauty to the measures which
tragic dialogue employs. Nearly two hundred
years earlier, Archilochus had given a majestic
rhythm to the trochaic tetrameter. A century
before Aeschylus, Solon had written iambic tri-
meters, among which there are at least some lines
not unworthy of Aeschylus himself. But it remained for the mighty spirit of Aeschylus to give
the iambic trimeter a sustained grandeur which
it had never possessed before. His style is always
the grand style ; yet it is not monotonous. He
can use iambic verse with equal mastery for terse
and vigorous narrative, as in describing the battle
of Salamis ; for declamation, as in the brilliant
rhetoric of Clytaemnestra, or the stately oration
of Athena; for concentrated invective, as when
Apollo drives the Furies from his temple ; for
keen controversy, as in the trial of Orestes ; or
for descriptive passages of tranquil beauty, as
when Prometheus depicts the change which he
had wrought on the primitive life of mankind.
Towards the end of the fifth century B. C., it became the fashion of a new school to censure Aeschylus as bombastic. The extant plays do not
justify the charge. They rather illustrate the

His style in
dialogue.

phrase applied to him by the Aristophanic chorus in the Frogs. He has the γηγενὲς φύσημα, the
breath of a Titan ; his strength sustains his grandeur ; he is often exuberant, but seldom turgid.

In the general view of the ancient world, Aeschylus was the supreme representative Ancient view
of dramatic inspiration, an inspiration of his genius.
sometimes too stormy and vehement to obey the
law of the best art. This feeling is crudely expressed in the tradition preserved by Athenaeus,
that Aeschylus wrote under the stimulus of wine,
and by the saying ascribed (falsely, we may well
believe) to Sophocles, that Aeschylus did right,
but without knowing why. The author of the
treatise on Sublimity attributed to Longinus similarly qualifies his estimate of the poet's genius.

To a modern mind, the most striking attribute
of Aeschylus is the lofty force of his cre- His creative
ative imagination. In the Eumenides, imagination.
for instance, every reader is aware of this, and
yet it is not easy for even the most appreciative
modern student to realize all that such an achievement signified. The Olympian gods and goddesses
were clearly defined forms, stronger and more beautiful men or women. But there were other supernatural beings whom the Greeks preferred to leave
in a reverent obscurity ; and of all such the most
appalling were the Erinyes. To call those dread
powers forth from the valley of the shadow into
the open light of day, to clothe them in a visible
shape, to show them in the very exercise of their

awful prerogatives, announcing their own name,
and asserting their office as avengers of blood, —
this was a thing which, among Greeks, only an
imagination of supreme boldness could have contemplated, and only an imagination of transcendent
power could have accomplished.

Hardly less bold, and not less wonderful, is the
feat achieved in the Prometheus. The only human
person in that play is Io, whose destiny separates
her from ordinary humanity. The other persons
are Prometheus, sprung from the race of the Titans
who had warred against Zeus, but himself one
whose wisdom had helped to establish the new
ruler's throne in heaven ; Oceanus, the earth-gir-
dling god of waters, borne through the air by a
winged creature to the Scythian wilderness where
Prometheus is chained to storm-beaten cliffs ; the
Ocean-Nymphs, daughters of Oceanus and Tethys ;
the god Hephaestus, whose satellites, Strength and
Force, aid him in executing the divine sentence ;
and Hermes, the messenger from Olympus. In
the drama which Aeschylus has made with such
beings, there is the sustained elevation which such
a theme required ; but there is also — and it is
the combination which is so peculiarly Hellenic —
a simplicity, a natural directness, which completes
the triumph. The imaginative surroundings of the
action are given with equal skill. There is no set
description, but a few hints or passing touches call
up a picture of the region in which Prometheus
suffers, — the sky above, the boundless sea far off

below, the desolate summits of the Caucasus between them; the frosty starlight of the nights, which only varied the torments of the victim; the driving snow, the raging wind, the thunderstorm and the earthquake. Vast and weird as is the vision, it is presented with Hellenic clearness of outline, with Hellenic obedience to the sense of measure and harmony.

In his principal human characters, Aeschylus exhibits the same creative force. Clytaemnestra is born whole from his brain; she *His conception of character.* becomes known through her deeds and words, till her presence can be felt; she acquires an atmosphere. How wonderfully her speech of welcome to Agamemnon, with its winding and glittering coils of rhetoric, makes us apprehend the hidden steadiness of her deadly purpose! And with what terrible reality does her exultation burst forth after the murder, in a series of short, sharp sentences, when she stands before the elders of Mycenae, telling them how the blood upon her robe has freshly spurted from her husband's death-wound, and how she rejoices in it, as a cornfield in the rains of spring! She is not merely the paramour of Aegisthus; she is the agent of the Erinys, who punishes Agamemnon for the slaughter of Iphigeneia. When she protests her confidence in the future, this is the sanction of her vow: "by the justice that has avenged my daughter, by Atè, and by the Fury, the powers to whom I have slain this man."

Like Clytaemnestra, each of the greater Aeschylean persons has an organic unity, shown
in action even more than through fine
touches of self-revealing speech. Universally, Aeschylus prefers action to speech, where
it is possible; in this direct sense he is the most
dramatic of the dramatists. The part of the Messenger is less indispensable to him than to his successors. No messenger relates the murder of Agamemnon; it is the dying man's shriek, heard by
the chorus from within, that announces the fulfil-
ment of Cassandra's vision. Action, not merely ex-
planatory dialogue or formal prologue, is his favorite opening for a play : the beacon flashes on the
watcher's gaze at Mycenae; the Pythia finds the
Eumenides in the temple, and the ghost of Clytaemnestra breaks their slumber.

Reference for action to speech.

In his theology, as in all else, Aeschylus is a
Hellene of the Hellenes : he is no mono-
theist, yet he might be described as a
monarchist in religion. Zeus is to him emphati-
cally the king of the gods. His Olympus is a
firmly ruled monarchy; for in the divine government of the world he finds a steadiness which implies unity of control; and, to the anthropomorphic
mind, this unity again implies a Supreme person.
Behind and above Zeus himself is Fate. Zeus,
says the Aeschylean Prometheus, is not the pilot
of Necessity. But we must recollect that Greek
polytheism had its historical perspective. The
dynasty of Zeus had succeeded to older dynasties.

His theology.

At the time when Prometheus spoke, Zeus was new to power ; Prometheus himself had helped to give him the victory, and Zeus was showing a kind of Olympian arrogance ; his new throne might still, in the workings of Fate, be shaken. This is, in fact, part at least of the answer to the problem which the Prometheus raises ; there had been faults on the side of Zeus no less than on the other, and therefore there was a ground of compromise. But such a danger for Zeus belonged to the remote past. Aeschylus would have allowed that a collision between Zeus and Fate was conceivable in the abstract, but would have denied, probably, that such a conflict lay any longer within the horizon of human religion. Zeus represents, for Aeschylus, the supreme rule of the world, so far as men can form any clear notion of it : —

"Zeus, whosoever he be, if this name please his ear,
    By this name I bid him hear;
    Nought but Zeus my soul may guess,   Agam.,
    Seeking far and seeking near,   160 ff., trans.
                                               by Ernest
    Seeking who shall stay the stress   Myers.
    Of its fond and formless fear."

And then follows an allusion to those two rulers who had preceded Zeus, namely, Uranus and Cronus : —

    "For he who long ago was great,
        Filled with daring and with might,
        Now is silent, lost in night ;
    And the next who took his state
Met *his* supplanter too, and fell, and passed from sight."

To the mind of Aeschylus, who had seen the overthrow of the Persian host, the divine judgment upon the violators of Hellenic shrines, Zeus was present not only as the god now established in supreme sway, but also as one who, in a far-off past, had striven against enemies, prevailed over competitors, beaten down the insolence of the earth-born.

Among the moral ideas which Aeschylus connects with religion, the dominant one is simple. It is the maxim, δράσαντι παθεῖν, the belief that sin must be expiated by suffering. Zeus has shown men the way to wisdom ; he has ordained that by suffering men shall learn. " Know this for thy children and thy house : as thou buildest, such in time shall be thy recompense." This idea takes a more complex form in the doctrine of the hereditary curse, the Erinys of the family. Laius, for instance, wrongs Pelops, and Pelops curses the race of Laius. Oedipus, the son of Laius, inherits that curse ; but an act of his own is required to call the Erinys into activity, and Oedipus unwittingly commits parricide and incest. Eteocles, the son of Oedipus, in turn sins against his father, and becomes subject to the curse. There is an element of mystic fatalism here, residing in the notion that a curse upon a whole race, once heard by the gods, will insure each successive generation acting in such a manner as to continue the operation of the Erinys. Aeschylus, we may suppose, simply accepted this

Retribution.

The transmitted curse.

belief. It is not probable that he had attempted
to effect in his own mind any logical reconciliation
between destiny and free will, much less that he
could have stated any theory which would have
stood the criticism of modern thought. This must
remain a matter of speculation ; but it is interesting to observe that as a poet he was unquestion-
ably influenced by his creed of retribution for sin,
and more particularly by the doctrine of the transmitted curse, in respect to his form of dramatic
composition. Welcker distinguishes two
kinds of trilogy used by Aeschylus. One *The trilogy.*
is the fable-trilogy, in which the three plays are
three successive chapters of one story, as the
Agamemnon, Choephori, Eumenides. The other
is the theme-trilogy, in which the bond between
the pieces is merely that of some general idea ;
thus the Supplices, according to Welcker, belonged
to a trilogy in which the connecting idea was that
of Hellenic victory over the barbarian. The evidence for the theme-trilogy is somewhat shadowy,
but there is no doubt that the fable-trilogy was
the form which Aeschylus, presumably its creator,
made distinctively his own. Now, the fable-trilogy
was evidently a congenial mode of composition for
a dramatist whose imagination was so spacious,
who loved to express character by great strokes
of action, and whose sympathy with the genius
of Homeric epos was so profound ; but the fable-
trilogy was also peculiarly suitable for the purpose of tracing the process by which, in the divine

counsels, sin is followed, soon or late, by suffering; above all, when the aim of the poet was to
show how the dread influence of the avenging
Fury, once established over a guilty house, descends from generation to generation.

From the founder of Tragedy we may now turn
Sophocles: to the poet who marks a further stage
his happy life. in its development. Sophocles was born
in or about 496 B. C., being thus some twenty-nine
years younger than Aeschylus. The ancient Greek
world can show no other man in whom all the elements of good fortune, as a Greek conceived them,
were united as they were in Sophocles. The gods,
whom he loved and who loved him, gave him physical beauty; rare genius; a sufficiency of wealth;
victories at the Dionysia, dating from his first
appearance as a competitor, and lasting down to
the end of a long life; distinction in the service
of his country; the affection of his fellow-citizens,
won by his character no less than by his achievements; an honored old age, in the full vigor of his
faculties; and a death which came at last oppor-
tunely, for by a few months only he was spared
hearing that cry, the dirge of the imperial city,
raised in the Peiraeus and caught up from point
to point through the line of the Long Walls, which
announced the overthrow at the Hellespont; he
was spared the sight of Athens besieged by a
Peloponnesian fleet, and finally occupied by a
Spartan garrison. Aeschylus had long ago died

in Sicily; Euripides had found a grave in Macedonia ; but Sophocles was laid to rest in his native land : and although embittered enemies were then established on Attic soil, their outposts respectfully opened a passage to the sad procession which moved along the road from Athens towards Deceleia, bearing the last of the great poets to the sepulchre of his fathers. A contemporary could thus sum up his life : —

> " Thrice happy Sophocles ! In good old age,
> Blessed as a man, and as a poet blessed,
> He died; his many tragedies were fair,
> And fair his end; nor knew he any sorrow."

The most important change made by Sophocles in the form of Tragedy consisted The third in raising the number of actors from actor. two to three. This was an innovation which Aeschylus could adopt, as in the Oresteia, without affecting the quality of his work ; but in the hands of Sophocles the change had large consequences. These cannot be understood until we have first considered the differences of thought concerning men and gods which separate Sophocles from Aeschylus. Here lies the root of the difference between the types of drama which they created.

Aeschylus had vindicated the ways of heaven to men by insistence upon the great Ethical and law which he regarded as all-pervading ; religious views of when a man suffers, it is a divine neme- Sophocles. sis upon sin. Zeus steadfastly upholds Righteousness. If you cannot discern how a sufferer has offended, or if his punishment seems too great for his offence, then go further back; search the history of his family; it will be found that somewhere there has been a sin. Thus the belief in destiny helped out the doctrine of retribution. Aeschylus put some strain on the facts of human experience, but at any rate he saved the justice of Zeus. Sophocles surveyed the spectacle of life with less prepossession and with a more tender sympathy. He was, like Aeschylus, a pious believer in the traditional religion of the Hellenes; but he held it in a form nearer to the received popular form than did Aeschylus. Zeus is not so steadily or uniformly paramount with Sophocles as he is with the elder poet. Apollo is often in the foreground, not as a mere mouthpiece of Zeus, but sometimes as a dispenser of good or ill. Athena, in the exercise of her own power, inflicts the chastisement upon Ajax. The idea of the hereditary curse is not strange to Sophocles; he sees it at work in the house of Pelops, in the house of Labdacus; but he makes it a less prominent agency than it is made by Aeschylus; it is enough to compare the Oedipus Tyrannus with the Seven against Thebes. As a rule, the Sophoclean person suffers either for what he himself has done — as Ajax for contempt of Athena — or else, being innocent, he suffers for no intelligible reason which the poet can assign, as Philoctetes does. The human lot is narrowly limited, and if a mortal trespasses on the limit, the jealousy of the gods will swiftly smite him. But more than this, Sophocles the fortunate can declare that never to be born is the best lot, and the next best, to die as soon as may be after birth. Life is the shadow of a vapor, and old age is misery. In a word, Sophocles is profoundly impressed with the woes of humanity, — woes which may be due to no fault of a man's own. Yet he firmly believes in the goodness and justice of the gods. He does not fall back on a half-mystic doctrine of nemesis. He leaves the problem unsolved. But he contributes at least one inestimable thought towards its solution. He teaches that suffering is not necessarily an evil. Suffering may educate and ennoble the character, as in the case of Oedipus. It may bring the victory of a cause which the sufferer prizes above life, as in the case of Antigone. Or, even if there can be nothing of comfort or compensation for the individual victim, his suffering may still have been ordained, in the hidden wisdom of just gods, for the good of mankind. Sophocles has been described, in well-known words, as one "who saw life steadily, and saw it whole." Those words, true of his dramatic art, are equally true of his religious and moral ideas. He saw the evil and sorrow that are in life as part of a divine scheme, which may, indeed, appoint such discipline for the good of the individual, but which also subordinates the welfare of the individual to the welfare of the race.

How, then, did such thoughts influence the work

of Sophocles as a dramatist? Aeschylus, with a
Influence of these ideas upon his art. grandeur and a breadth akin to those of heroic epos, showed the heroes in the great outlines of their action, fulfilling the destiny appointed for them by Zeus, and illustrating the eternal law of Righteousness. Sophocles believed not less in the fixity of the divine law; but he dwelt on less simple forms of its operation: when he contemplated human passions and sufferings, he felt the apparent contradictions to divine goodness, though his faith in that goodness was profound. Hence his human sympathy on the one side and his piety on the other conspired to interest him in character, in the motives and feelings of men, in the influences which they exert over each other, and in the effects upon them of the divine discipline. Here he saw the best hope of resolving the apparent discords.

The chief formal change which he made in Tragedy aided him in working out this tendency of his mind. A third actor made it possible to exhibit the interaction of human motives with greater subtlety and fullness. The dialogue now became still more important than Aeschylus had made it. The Chorus lost nothing of its value in the lyric province; but it ceased to take so active a part in the drama. The trilogy remained the usual, if not the imperative, form of tragic production. But Sophocles usually dispensed with a link of story between the three plays. Here, again, his distinctive aim interprets his practice.

In an Aeschylean trilogy, such as the *Oresteia,*
the unity of the trilogy supersedes that of the
single play. Sophocles prefers a more limited
framework, within which the finer touches of
ethical portraiture can be appreciated.

Plutarch briefly notices three stages of development through which the manner of So-
phocles had passed, and ascribes the The three periods of his style.
account to the poet himself. What his
authority may have been, we do not know. But
the three stages are in themselves probable, and
part, at least, of the development can be traced in
the extant plays. In the first stage, Sophocles is
said to have imitated the grandeur of Aeschylus.
The phrase used by Plutarch implies that in this
grandeur the younger poet came to feel something
crude and immature. There is other evidence
besides this for the tradition that Sophocles,
while regarding Aeschylus as a sublimely inspired poet, was conscious of his own superiority
as an artist. The second stage in his style was
marked, according to Plutarch, by a certain arti-
ficiality; — by elaborate art which had not yet mas-
tered the secret of concealing itself. In his third
and final phase, Sophocles had perfected and
mellowed the best style for the dramatic expression of character. The final goal here indicated,
as that towards which the poet's whole development had moved, is certainly the true one; the
fine delineation of human character in action
was the supreme and distinctive excellence of

Sophocles. It cannot be said that in the extant plays there is any trace of the first, or Aeschylean phase. But when the Antigone, produced probably in 441 B. C., is compared with the Philoctetes, produced thirty-two years later (in 409 B. C.), we can discern some traces of a progress from the second phase to the third. The portraiture of character in the Antigone is, indeed, already consummate. But the style of composition is slightly more artificial than in the Philoctetes ; and the Antigone, though probably the earliest of the extant plays, was produced when the poet was at least fifty-five, and when he had been at work for twenty-seven years. If we possessed plays written before the Antigone, and belonging to the period from 468 to 441 B. C., the steps of the progress could doubtless be more clearly traced.

In a Sophoclean tragedy there is always some central issue, so contrived as to probe the depths of character in the principal agents. In the Antigone, for example, it is the conflict between the resolve of Antigone to obey the unwritten law of the gods by burying her brother, and the resolve of Creon to enforce his own edict against the burial. And it is the poet's strong grasp of this situation which gives a vital unity to the whole drama. The issue is set forth in a conversation between Antigone and her sister Ismene, with which the play begins. This is the type of opening adopted by Sophocles

Characteristics of a Sophoclean play.

in all the extant plays; for the Trachiniae is not really an exception, although the speech with which Deianeira opens it so far resembles a prologue of Euripides as to be historical. These initial conversations, it should be observed, do not merely explain the situation from which the action starts; they also illustrate the character of some principal person — as that of Antigone. The march of a Sophoclean drama corresponds with the strength and clearness of the central conception; it never halts, though its course is diversified by variety of incident. Thus in the Antigone we have the scenes between Creon and the guard set to watch the corpse; between Creon and his son Haemon, who intercedes for Antigone; between Creon and the prophet Teiresias, who foretells the divine wrath. Every occurrence, every speech, contributes to the dramatic progress; at every step the tragic interest rises towards the climax. The Chorus directly assists this progress; not indeed, as a rule, by sharing in the action, The Sophoclean Chorus. but by attuning the thoughts of the spectators to successive moods in sympathy with the action of the play. Thus in the Antigone the subjects of the six choral odes are, the past peril of Thebes from the Argive allies of Polyneices; the audacity of man, as illustrated by the unknown breaker of Creon's edict, who has given burial to Polyneices; the power of love, as shown by Haemon's intercession; the prisons of Danaë,

Lycurgus, and Cleopatra, as compared with the rock-tomb which awaits Antigone ; and the beneficence of Dionysus, whom the Chorus, in a brief gleam of delusive hope, summon to share in the anticipated joy of his favorite Thebes. Each of these six themes has a direct bearing on the dramatic moment.

The poetry of Sophocles is the expression of a mind in which the happiest natural gifts had been ripened during the happiest years of Athenian history. It had been the work of Pericles, between 460 and 430 B. C., to realize the essential idea of a Greek city as it had never been realized before. The Athenian citizen, rich or poor, could now take his part in the public life of the city without undue sacrifice of his private interests, and could also participate in the noblest pleasures of literature and art. Forms of beauty were around him which, in the words ascribed to Pericles, gave a daily delight that banished gloom. Two men who lived in that age are above all others its witnesses to the modern world. The mind of Thucydides had been moulded by the ideas of Pericles, and doubtless by personal intercourse with him ; the Periclean stamp can be recognized in the clearness with which Thucydides apprehends that the vital thing for a state is less the pattern of its constitution than the spirit in which it is governed. Sophocles, again, as a dramatist, shows the Periclean influence in his manner of investing

Sophocles and the Age of Pericles.

the traditions of Hellenic religion with a higher
spiritual and intellectual meaning, and more generally in the harmonious perfection of his poetical
art. The artistic side of the Periclean age is
indeed represented by the plays of Sophocles in
literature, as by the Parthenon in architecture and
sculpture. Sophoclean tragedy exhibits the same
union of power with purity of taste, the same
self-restraint, the same instinct of symmetry,
which can still be admired in the remains of the
temple. In the poetry, as in the marble, the
Athenian spirit shows the fineness to which it
could be tempered by the concurrence of those
influences and conditions which the age of Pericles
had brought together, — a fortunate union which
could not have occurred at any earlier moment,
and which, when these few years had passed, was
never repeated.

The greatness of Sophocles as a poet depends
primarily on his greatness as an artist. Among
his gifts, those to which he chiefly owes his fame
are, his sympathetic insight, his unfailing sense
of proportion and harmony, his chastened beauty
of workmanship, — in a word, those faculties by
which he renders Tragedy a perfect work of ideal
art. Aeschylus takes rank, not primarily in virtue of such gifts as these, but more distinctively
by his sublime imaginative vision. The glory
which surrounded Sophocles at Athens for more
than sixty years attests the high level of mental
cultivation and of artistic feeling which then pre-

vailed among Athenians, — not among a select
few only, but in those audiences of twenty thousand or more which filled the theatre at the
Dionysia. It is not to be expected that modern
readers generally should appreciate Sophocles so
readily as Aeschylus. With modern readers,
Aeschylus has, to begin with, one momentous
advantage; there is a strain in his poetry, due to
his doctrine concerning the divine vindication of
righteousness, which gives him some measure of
resemblance to a Hebrew prophet. Sophocles,
on the other hand, subjects the modern mind to
the severest test of a capacity for appreciating
the purely Hellenic spirit in its highest form.
The degree in which a modern enjoys Sophocles
is not necessarily a measure of his feeling for
poetry; but it may fairly be taken as a measure
of his sympathy with the finest qualities of the
Athenian genius.

The third master of Attic Tragedy must be
reserved for separate treatment.

VII

THE ATTIC DRAMA (*continued*)

THE victory at Salamis, in which Aeschylus took part as a soldier, and which Sopho- Euripides. cles, as leader of the boy-chorus, helped to celebrate, marks the birth-year of Euripides. Like Aeschylus, he competed for the tragic prize at the age of twenty-five, but had to wait many years before he gained it. His first success was in 441, when he was thirty-nine; and in a career of nearly half a century that success was only four times repeated. To the end of his days he was the butt of Attic Comedy, which, besides ridiculing his plays, propagated all manner of stories concerning his private life. He was a lonely man, a student and a thinker, who lived in seclusion, — a strong contrast, here, to Aeschylus the soldier and Sophocles the man of affairs. It was an old tradition that he had fitted up a place of study in a cave on the shore of Salamis, where he used to work, looking out upon the sea; and much of his imagery is taken, not indeed from the sea itself, but from the life of seafarers. He was a friend of Anaxagoras, to whom he has paid a beautiful tribute (fr. 910, ὄλβιος κ. τ. λ.). His management of controversy bears the impress of Protagoras. No tradition associates him with the circle of

Pericles; nor does any trace in his work show the influence of Socrates.

The relation of Euripides to the Athens of his time has two distinct aspects, both of which are illustrated by his plays. On the intellectual side, he was in general sympathy with the tendencies which prevailed during the second half of his career. The rhetorical dialectic of the new teachers, with its sophistical subtleties, is conspicuous in his writings. He alludes here and there to particular opinions of various thinkers — Heracleitus, Xenophanes, Anaxagoras — in a manner which indicates his speculative bent ; but he is not a declared adherent of any school; nor yet has he a definite philosophy of his own. The central point of his ethical doctrine is the importance of the individual's nature, φύσις, his intellectual and moral endowment. He has not broken, meanwhile, with the popular religion ; he claims to criticise it freely in the light of morality and reason.

His relation to contemporary Athens.

Thus far he was fairly in accord with the tone of his age ; but on the social and political side it was otherwise. Nothing in his work shows the intellectual stamp of the Periclean age — as the work of Sophocles, for instance, shows it by the desire to reconcile consecrated tradition with a higher range of thought. Euripides is not, like Sophocles, a true child of that age. His aspirations were rather those, in modern phrase, of philosophical radicalism ; he longed for a form of democracy in which the reign of reason should be still less fettered by prescription. The death of Pericles, in 429, removed a great moderating power ; but Euripides had the pain of seeing the democracy, when freed from that strong hand, degrade liberty into license, and drown the voice of sober counsel in the strife of demagogues. He shrank from this debased democracy. His best word is for the small farmer, who seldom comes to town, and who does not soil his rustic honesty by contact with the crowd of the market-place. For a while, indeed, Euripides had one bright hope : it was the young and dazzling Alcibiades, for whose victory in the Olympian chariot-race (420 B. C.) he composed the last recorded example of the epinikion. Might not Alcibiades become a second Pericles, only with more advanced aims ? That hope was cruelly disappointed. About 409 B. C. Euripides left Athens : and he was not destined to return. He went to king Archelaus in Macedonia. In the rough military world of that half-barbarian court, Euripides, now just seventy, would have met a younger Athenian dramatist, Agathon. The wild scenery of the northern land is reflected in the Bacchae. He died there in the winter of 407–406 B. C.

The dramatic work of Euripides interests alike by its success and by its failure. It is the most instructive of comments on the nature of Attic Tragedy, and on the limits which that nature imposed. It is also fraught with the His works as a dramatist.

germs of a new drama; it is the source of influences which proved fruitful in the later literature
of antiquity; it is even a link between the ancient
and the modern theatre. But few literary questions are more difficult to estimate fairly than the
relation of Euripides to a form of art which he
enriched with some of its noblest ornaments, but
on which he also impressed tendencies that could
lead only to decay and extinction.

Tragedy came to Euripides with its general conditions fixed in a manner which he could
not attempt to alter. Three actors, a
chorus, subject-matter to be taken from the heroic
legends, — these were the essentials. Aeschylus
and Sophocles, unlike in so much, were alike in
this, that to the external traditions of their drama
they had added an unwritten law as to its spirit,
which they both observed with unwavering con-
stancy : it was that the treatment should be ideal.
Agamemnon, for example, was not to be taken out
of the heroic atmosphere with which the myth surrounded him. He was, indeed, to be made living;
but the life was to be that of a Greek hero, —
in other words, of a man belonging to the far-
off age when gods mingled in the warfare on the
plain of Troy; a man, moreover, directly descended
from Zeus himself. The divine light which played
around that age was compatible with the full humanity of the heroes, as it is in the Iliad, only the
humanity must be noble. That nobleness is independent of rank or circumstance. The Homeric

Tragedy had been ideal.

swineherd Eumaeus has it as well as Achilles.
The necessary minimum of such nobleness might
be defined negatively. Persons whose life is placed
in the heroic age must not so act or speak as to
resemble ordinary men or women of the contemporary world. If they do so, they may be interesting, but they lose their ideal character. By
ceasing to be ideal they also become, as heroic
persons, less real. Agamemnon, arguing like an
astute lawyer or an ingenious demagogue, may
be a more familiar type of person, but the illusion
that we are listening to the king of Mycenae is
ruined.

Now Euripides was a poet fertile in ideas, full
of views on all the questions of his day,
— religious, moral, political, social. If he
was to write Tragedy, he could only use the heroic
myths. Tragedy was an act of worship. He could
not be allowed to write a tragedy about Miltiades
or Themistocles; but when he had chosen his heroic *dramatis personae*, the impulse was irresistible
to make these persons the exponents of his teem-
ing thoughts on contemporary life. "It was easy
enough for Aeschylus," we can imagine him saying, "to exclude modern thought; there were no
pressing problems then; the era of reason had
scarcely dawned; besides his poetical vision, Aeschylus had only his half-mystic theology, which
suited it. It is easy, too, for worthy Sophocles, a
pious soul who lives for art, not for philosophy;
but if *I* am to give the people of my best, — if I

The problem for Euripides.

am to teach and improve them through my poetry at the Dionysia, — how can I keep within those old limits of conventional utterance?"

So Euripides went to work in his own new

His mode of solving it.

way. The extent to which he modernized the heroes must not be exaggerated. He observed measure. Still, he introduced a most vital change; he brought the diction and thought of the heroic persons far nearer to that of every-day life; he added small traits of character, which, in contrast to the finer touches of Sophocles, did not (as a rule) deepen the significance of those persons, but merely made them appear more commonplace. And, pervading his plays, there was what must be called the sophistical strain, most prominent in the Protagorean rhetoric of the debates, where λόγος is pitted against λόγος, but seen also in the remarks on the gods, or on moral questions. Here the light of common day was let in upon the heroic age, with disastrous results for dramatic effect. A new treatment of the Chorus

The Chorus.

was an inevitable consequence. In this respect the difference between Aeschylus and Sophocles had been less important than the agreement: both had maintained the organic bond between Chorus and dialogue. This was possible, because the animating spirit of their dialogue was one which could be continued in lyric utterance; it was noble; it belonged to the age of the heroes. But after a

dialogue in which two disputants had displayed
the latest novelties of rhetorical casuistry, how
could a choral ode be in accord with it? And
besides this difficulty, there was a positive motive for a change — the wish for variety. Thus
the choral odes of Euripides came to be either
wholly irrelevant to the dramatic context, or
connected with it only slightly and occasionally.

The instinct which told Euripides that the
day of Attic Tragedy, as the elder masters had
understood it, could not be much prolonged, was
a true one; the signs were around him. But
it is a different question, and one not easily
answered, how far he actually felt, in his last
twenty or thirty years, the pressure of a public
demand, which his innovations were designed to
meet. It is a significant fact that, in 409 B. C.,
when the career of Euripides was nearing its
close, the Philoctetes of Sophocles gained the first
prize. The old style of Tragedy could still hold
its own, then, with the public — at least in the
hands of Sophocles. But the veteran
poet may have been a favored exception. Certainly there are several features in
the work of Euripides which look like concessions
to a new popular taste. Foremost among these
is his adoption in his lyrics of the musical novelties associated with the new dithyrambic school,
and especially with Timotheus. The
general tendency of these was to substitute a florid style, with profuse ornament, for the

simpler and purer music of the older Tragedy.
A step in the same direction was the monody, — a
solo sung by an actor, who accompanied it with
an expressive dance.   Such monodies — called
"Cretan" by Aristophanes, since the dance was
of Cretan origin — were elements of operatic
ballet thrust into Greek Tragedy.   Outside of
the lyric province, an appeal to popular taste
may be surmised in the love of Euripides for
Mechanical   startling effects in the management of
effects.   the plot.   The use of the *deus ex ma-
china* was often, doubtless, merely to cut a knot ;
but we may conjecture that it was also popular
in itself, as a ghost is always popular on the modern stage.   The Euripidean prologue, introducing
the spectators to the subject of the play, was
again a boon to ignorance or mental indolence.

In such particulars, the course adopted by
General scope   Euripides may have been prescribed, or
of his changes.   favored, by his audiences.   But the essence of his reform, at any rate, had little to do
with popular taste.   He was not driven to it ; he
imposed it.   The wit of Aristophanes often packs
a great deal of sound criticism into a few words.
His Euripides says that, when he received Tragedy from Aeschylus, it was plethoric, swollen,
and heavy.   He treated it for this malady, giving
it decoctions which reduced it to a leaner but
more healthy state.   Then he proceeded to feed
it up again, with such a stimulating diet as monodies.   There is a biting truth in this mockery.

Euripides had to apply the principle of compensation. The heroic had to be replaced by the sensational.

In attempting to estimate the work of Euripides, we must indeed guard against allowing too much weight to the verdict of Attic Comedy; but neither can we ignore it. It is necessary to apprehend the point of view from which this contemporary satire assailed him, *Antagonism of the Comic Poets.* and the grounds on which it based its unfavorable judgment. If we then proceed to modify that judgment in the light of a larger survey, we shall do so with less fear of erring through modern misconception.

The hostility of Aristophanes to Euripides was certainly bitter; nor can it surprise us, if he believed Euripides to have done all the mischief with which he charges him. But Aristophanes was not the only comic poet who attacked Euripides. There was a deeper reason for this than any individual or personal *Ultimate cause of this.* sentiment. Attic Comedy had a natural quarrel with the innovator in Tragedy, and the ground of this lay in its own history.

Sicily is one of two regions in which the origin of Comedy is to be sought; the other is Athens. The Dorians, both in Sicily *Development of Attic Comedy.* and in Greece proper, early showed a bent towards farcical humor; in the case of the Siceliots, there may have been Italic influences at work, since it has always been an Italic gift to

seize those traits of life and character which suit
farce and burlesque. At the courts of the Sicilian princes such entertainments were welcome.
The Dorian Epicharmus, from the Sicilian Megara, was the first who developed the ruder farce
into a species of dramatic poetry. This was done
at Syracuse, where the tragic poets Phrynichus
and Aeschylus had been the guests of Hieron;
and Attic Tragedy may have suggested the general idea of the form which Epicharmus adopted,
though he does not seem to have used a Chorus.
Athens, during the same period—the first half
of the fifth century B. C.—developed a comic
drama from a different source. At the Dionysia, when the people were assembled to worship the god and to see tragedy, the merry
procession called a *comus* had become a recognized feature of the festival. It was at first a
voluntary and unofficial affair. One or more
troops of men dressed themselves up in mummers'
costume, and marched into the sacred precinct
to the music of the flute. They then sang a song
in honor of Dionysus; and one of their number
addressed the audience in a humorous speech,
turning on civic interests and on the topics of
the day. The festal procession then withdrew
again. The name Comedy, κωμῳδία, originally
denoted this "Song of the Comus," and was
doubtless coined at Athens, on the analogy of
tragoedia. About 465 B. C. the *comus* was adopted
into the official programme of the festival: in-

stead of being the voluntary work of private
persons, it was now organized with aid from the
State. The steps by which a dramatic performance was built up around the comus-song and
speech can no longer be traced. But some five
and thirty years later, at the beginning of the
Peloponnesian war, Attic Comedy, as we know
it, was mature. Tragedy naturally furnished the
general model on which the new kind of drama
was constructed. This is apparent in the limit
placed on the number of actors; no extant play
of Aristophanes requires more than three regular
actors, allowance being made for small parts
being taken by supernumeraries who were not
required to be absolutely mute. But Comedy
was connected with Tragedy by much more than
this kinship of form. Comedy expressed the
frolicsome side of that Dionysiac worship from
which Tragedy took its birth. Religion, the
religion of Dionysus, was the breath of life to
Comedy, not less — perhaps even more — than
to her grave sister. It was religion that author-
ized the riot of fancy which turns the world
topsy-turvy, the jests upon all things Olympian
or human, the unsparing personal satire. Let
that popular religion once lose its hold, and
then, though Tragedy might survive, Comedy,
such as Aristophanes wrote, must lose its sacred
privileges, and, with them, its reason for existing. By the first law of its being, the Old
Comedy was the sworn foe of all things which

could undermine the sway of Dionysus, the god
who not only inspires the poet, but protects his
liberties.   And the nearer Tragedy stood to the
original form which the Dionysiac cult had given
to it, the closer was the kinship which Comedy
felt with it.   For this reason Aeschylus represents, even better than Sophocles, the form of
Tragedy with which the muse of Aristophanes
was in spiritual accord; and Euripides represents everything which that muse abhors.   Euripides, who dwarfs the heroic stature, and pro-
fanes heroic lips with the rhetoric of the Ecclesia
or the law-court; Euripides, with his rationalism,
his sophistry, his proclivity to new-fangled notions
of every kind — here Comedy, with sure instinct,
saw a dramatist who was using the Dionysia
against the very faith to which that festival was
devoted, and whose poetry was the subtle solvent
by which Comedy and Tragedy alike were destined
to perish.

It was a happy fortune that, before its short
life came to an end, the essence of Attic
Comedy was so perfectly expressed by
the great satirist who was also a great poet.   The
genius of Aristophanes indeed transcends the
form in which he worked; but it exhibits all
the varied capabilities of that form.   He can
denounce a corrupt demagogue or an unworthy
policy with a stinging scorn and a force of righteous indignation which make the poet almost
forgotten in the patriot.   He can use mockery

Aristophanes.

with the lightest touch. But it is not in denun-
ciation or in banter that his most exquisite faculty
is revealed. It is rather in those lyric passages
where he soars above everything that can move
laughter or tears, and pours forth a strain of such
free, sweet music and such ethereal fancy as it
would be hard to match save in Shakespeare. A
poet who united such gifts brought keen insight
and fine taste to the task of the critic.

In reading the Frogs, we do not forget that it
is a comedy, not a critical essay. And The criticism
we allow for the bias against Euripides. in the Frogs.
But no careful student of the play can fail to ad-
mire how Aristophanes seizes the essential points
in the controversy between the two schools of
Tragedy. When Aeschylus has said that a poet
ought to edify, Euripides rejoins (in effect), "Are
you edifying when you indulge in dark grandilo-
quence, instead of explaining yourself in the language of ordinary humanity?" Now observe
the rejoinder of Aeschylus. He replies, "Great
sentiments and great thoughts are suitably clothed
in stately words. Besides, it is natural that the
demigods (τοὺς ἡμιθέους) should have grandeur of
words; for their clothes are much grander than
ours. I exhibited all this properly — and you
have utterly spoiled it." Here Aristophanes has
put the true issue in a simple form. Aeschylus
is right in vindicating his own style, and con-
demning his rival's, by an appeal to the nature
of his subject-matter. Heroes and demigods

ought not to speak like ordinary men. He is right, too, when he enforces his point by referring to the stately costume which he had devised for Tragedy. This was a visible symbol of the limit set to realism.

When Aristophanes passes from the ground of art to that of ethics, the justice of his criticism may be less evident to moderns, but here also he is substantially right from the Athenian point of view. His Aeschylus complains that Euripides had sapped the springs of civic manliness, of patriotism, and even of morality. It is true that Euripides, as a dramatic poet, had contributed to tendencies setting in that direction. Homer had been regarded by the Greeks as their greatest teacher, because the heroes were the noblest ideals of human life which they possessed. Aeschylus and Sophocles, in their different ways, had preserved the Homeric spirit. If the heroes once ceased to be ideals of human life, the ordinary Greek of the fifth century had no others. To depose the heroes from their elevation above commonplace humanity was also to destroy an indispensable link between god and man in the popular religion. But that religion was at the root of the Greek citizen's loyalty to the city.

In the smaller details of his polemic against Euripides, the comic poet is sometimes acute and just, sometimes excessively unfair. We are not here concerned with such details. The broad facts which claim our atten-

Summary.

tion are simply these. Attic Comedy, as such, was the natural foe of a tragic poet like Euripides. Aristophanes clearly understood the artistic limits proper to Attic Tragedy. He clearly saw where and how Euripides had transgressed them ; he also saw that this error of Euripides in art was, for the Athens of his day, inseparable from a bad moral influence. And Aristophanes can sum up his judgment by saying that Euripides, in pursuing new refinements, had abandoned the greatest things (τὰ μέγιστα) of the Tragic Art — as Athens had known it.

The very qualities by which Euripides incurred this censure endeared him to later antiquity, both Greek and Roman. As Attic Tragedy perished with Euripides, so the old life of Athens, and of Hellas itself, perished only seventy years later. Hellas gave place to Hellenism, a civilization in which Hellenic and foreign elements were mingled. This later Greek age recognized Euripides as its prophet. He had been before his own time, and therefore he was in harmony with theirs. In touching the deep problems of human destiny, he had given utterance to their scepticism, perplexity, melancholy. In drawing human character, he had used a thousand subtle touches which every day they could recognize as true, and which they found in no other poet of old Hellas. He delighted them by the bold ingenuity of his plots and by the brilliant beauty of his descriptions.

Popularity of Euripides in later times;

Hellenistic;

He was with them, too, in their sorrows; if any one of them had been visited by a cruel reverse of fortune, or by a heart-breaking bereavement, he could find no poet whose sympathy was so human as that of Euripides, or who could so gently unseal the fountain of tears. And therefore Euripides became indeed their idol. He was the inspiration, and in much the pattern, of the new Attic Comedy. One of its poets, Philemon, exclaims, "If the dead retain their senses, as some say, I would hang myself to see Euripides."

At Rome, from the latter part of the third century B. C. onwards, he was equally welcome. Ennius translated the Medea; Pacuvius and Attius took him for their chief model. The Parthian Orodes was seeing a performance of the Bacchae, when the actor who was playing Agavè produced the gory head of Crassus. Dante, who does not name Aeschylus or Sophocles, numbers Euripides among the great poets of Greece. In the period of the Renaissance Euripides was more popular than either of the elder dramatists. Racine was his disciple; and his influence predominates in Milton's "Samson Agonistes." It has been his crowning good fortune in modern times that, when a reaction against him came, towards the end of the last century, the reaction was intemperate. Such excessive disparagement as Schlegel's elicited a protest from Goethe, who says that it is absurd to deny sublimity to Euripides,

[marginal notes: Roman; mediaeval; and modern.]

and that "if a modern man must pick out faults in so great an ancient, he ought to do it upon his knees." This is one of those generous outbursts which are sure of applause; and yet the defense is not relevant. No intelligent criticism would deny that Euripides is sometimes sublime; he is so, incontestably, in the Bacchae. Nevertheless modern criticism has a right to speak, though it should be reverent. Euripides has qualities which place him among the world's great poets and fully justify all the admiration which he has won from posterity. But these qualities must also be estimated relatively to the form and to the age in which he worked. The conflict of modern judgments upon him has arisen in large measure from failing to keep the two points of view distinct.

Some of his best plays charm the modern reader, not merely by particular beau- Intrinsic ties, but also by unity of effect. Such are merits of Euripides the Medea, the Hippolytus, the Ion, the as a poet. Bacchae. But it is distinctive of Euripides, as compared with Aeschylus and Sophocles, that the interest of particular passages is usually felt more strongly than the harmony of the whole. There are powerful scenes, which can often be detached. There are ideas, maxims, sentiments, of which it is easy to make an anthology. In an age of intellectual and moral unsettlement, a cultivated man who gives a voice to each doubt or emotion as it arises is certain to have the ear of posterity. It is not only in action that history repeats itself.

At one point or another, in this phase or that of
his reflections, Euripides has a kinship with the
troubled spirits of every race and century. Not
less universal in its appeal to the modern mind
is that gleam of romance which he makes to play,
with so strange a beauty, around the shapes of
classical mythology. We see it in the story of
Phaedra, pining with secret love; in the story of
Ion, the young ministrant of the Delphian temple,
who comes to learn the secret of his parentage;
in both the plays concerning the fortunes of Iphigeneia. This tinge of romance is given chiefly
by two things, — analysis of the individual's feeling, aided by minute portraiture of circumstance,
and sudden surprises in the plot, — sometimes
through supernatural agency. But a romantic
coloring is not the only quality of Euripides in
which he might be regarded as a precursor of
modern drama. In one play at least, the Bacchae,
he shows a sense of natural beauty, lit up by
fancy, which no other Greek poet, perhaps, has
manifested with equal splendor. The same play
is also distinguished from all the other works of
its author by profound sympathy with the spirit
of the Dionysiac worship. It was written in
Macedonia shortly before his death; and might
almost have propitiated Aristophanes himself, who
very likely had not seen it when he wrote the
Frogs.

Euripides was sometimes reproached with the
tearful scenes in his plays. His critics called him

maudlin and effeminate. He has made a good answer, and it is curiously modern. The disguised Orestes is deeply moved by the plight in which he finds his sister Electra. As he is supposed to be a stranger, he feels it necessary to make some excuse for his emotion, lest it should surprise her. " Pity," he says, " nowhere dwells with ignorance, but with the wise among men ; for indeed the wise have to pay a price for their advantage in wisdom." "Wise," " wisdom," here refer to mental cultivation. He means that sensibility to the sight of suffering is the proof, and the penalty, of mental refinement.

There is yet another trait in the poetry of Euripides which often gives it a peculiar charm for moderns. Though he was called a misogynist, no one has shown a finer appreciation of feminine tenderness or feminine strength. Nor has any ancient poet given more beautiful expression to the family affections. Take, for instance, this fragment of the Erechtheus : " Love your mother, children, for there is no love that it is sweeter to cherish." In another fragment (No. 909) a devoted wife is very beautifully described. She holds her husband's affection by her goodness more surely than by beauty ; she looks always on the bright side of his deeds and words ; his troubles and joys are reflected in her countenance ; she helps to bear his burdens, and without feeling it to be a pain. It is significant that these verses have been preserved by a Christian writer, Clement of Alexandria.

Such are the qualities by which Euripides became the first prophet of a cosmopolitan humanity. His influence on the history of the world has been wider than that of either Aeschylus or Sophocles, for the interests and feelings to which he appeals are common to all men. He demands no peculiar sympathy with the Hellenic spirit ; he makes no severe demand on the historical imagination. No sane criticism would now dispute his claim to a place among the world's great poets.

Yet the serious student of Greek literature must not shrink from a difficult and almost painful duty ; he must not shut his eyes to the truth that Aristophanes was right in the main, both artistically and morally. This great and fascinating poet, Euripides, the author of a dazzling compromise, the precursor of the romantic drama, was not a sound Hellenic artist ; he was a herald of death to the art around which he threw those novel splendors. In modern phrase, we may say that Tragedy as he found it was ideal, and that his tendency was towards realism ; only, in using those words, we must remember that the Greek mind, when it was at its best, — as it was in the middle of the fifth century B. C., — knew no such antithesis between idealism and realism in art as our use of those terms is apt to suggest. Achilles, for instance, was what we should call an ideal to the Greeks ; he was so, however, not as transcending humanity, not as a semi-abstract person seen

Euripides as tried by the Hellenic standard.

His "realism:" what it meant.

through a divine mist, but because he was so
lucidly and brilliantly human, — human in the
most splendid and pathetic shape that Greek fancy
could give to a young hero.   Odysseus was an
ideal as being a man, vividly drawn, of superlative
fortitude, ability, and resource.   When Euripides
made such persons speak in the strain of contemporary rhetoric or casuistry, he was not making
them, from a Greek point of view, more real ; he
was making them, considered as heroes, less so,
because he was reducing them from a higher to a
lower sphere of reality.   Menander did not feel
this, any more than the ordinary modern reader
does, because in Menander's day the old Hellenic
life was broken up, and the old faith was dead ;
but Aristophanes felt it, and Sophocles would have
felt it too.   Sophocles, in his later years, experi-
enced the influence of Euripides on the technical
side, — in some details of composition and versifi-
cation, — though not to the extent that has sometimes been assumed ; but no one can say that in
the essence of his conception — in "the greatest things" of the tragic art, as Aristophanes
calls them — Sophocles ever made the smallest
approach to the younger poet's manner.   The
lines of an English poetess are well known : —

> "Our Euripides the human
>   With his droppings of warm tears,
> And his touching of things common
>   Till they rise to meet the spheres."

The last two lines may often be as true for *us*

as the first two; but they do not truly describe what Euripides did for those of his Athenian contemporaries who were in sympathy with the traditional Hellenic faith. In their view, he so touched things heroic as to make them, — not rise to meet the spheres, — but descend nearer to the level of common ground. Cicero, in an eloquent passage,[1] has pleaded for aesthetic tolerance on the ground of the wide differences of individual type between artists who excel in the same field. Sculpture is a single art, he says; and yet how unlike each other are Myron, Polycleitus, and Lysippus! Painting is a single art; and yet there is little resemblance between Zeuxis, Aglaophon, and Apelles. It is so also, he proceeds, in poetry. Roman literature presents us with the contrasts of Ennius, Pacuvius, and Attius; Greek literature, with those of Aeschylus, Sophocles, and Euripides. This is an excellent instance of a plausible criticism which moderns would be apt to accept as almost a truism, and which, nevertheless, so far as Greek art and poetry are concerned, misses the vital point. The difference between Myron and Polycleitus in Greek sculpture is utterly different, not merely in degree but in kind, from that which both present in relation to Lysippus. Aeschylus and Sophocles are dissimilar; but the difference is not the same in kind as that which divides both of them from Euripides.

In the highest Greek genius, symmetry and har-

[1] De Oratore, 3. 7. § 26.

mony were essential elements; the Hellene had established a concord of spirit and body which he impressed upon the creations of his mind, and in which resides the *The great age of Greek poetry;* peculiar secret of their beauty; therefore the truly classical poetry of Greece, such as that of Homer, Pindar, Aeschylus, Sophocles, cannot be understood, — indeed, is not conceivable, — apart from the phase of Hellenic society and Hellenic thought in which each kind had its birth ; to each of them this society and this thought were necessary conditions.

At the end of the fifth century before Christ the intellectual progress of Hellas had produced a discord between the inward *and the decline.* and the outward life which nothing could have resolved, short of some new religion which should succeed to the place of the old. And, as this discord became ever more conscious and more complex, the framework of the outward life itself was dissolved ; there came a divorce between society and the state ; the citizen no longer lived for the city. It is no accident that the creative period of the Greek mind closed with the end of the old social and political order in Hellas. Studious leisure might remain ; learning might increase ; new regions of knowledge might be opened; but the highest inspiration of literature and of art had disappeared.

It may be urged on behalf of Euripides that, without some such changes as he introduced, Tragedy could no longer hope to please. The altered circumstances of the time demanded

The course taken by Euripides.

the concession. This may be granted, at least for the time immediately after his : but it is only another way of saying that Attic Tragedy had reached the term of its existence, as Ionian epos had done at an earlier date. A great poet in whom the artistic sense was more purely Hellenic than it was in Euripides would have refrained from attempting a compromise. He would have felt that the result, however effective, could not be harmonious ; that not merely would the form of Attic Tragedy be modified, but its very soul would be extinguished.

The historical proof of this is given by the

Its literary sequel.

actual development of Greek drama after Euripides. Tragedy languished in a feeble imitative way, and soon ceased altogether. It was in the line of Comedy that the work begun by the last of the tragic masters was continued and completed. The portraiture of ordinary character, the realistic description of ordinary life, to which Euripides had made the first approach, reached its full development in the New Comedy.

Menander.

Menander was as far from the lofty lyric strain of Aristophanes as from his wild fantasy and his personal satire. Menander's prevailing tone was that of polite conversation ; not without passages of tender sentiment, grave thought, or almost tragic pathos. Thus his style was nearly on the level to which

Euripides had reduced Tragedy : the resemblance was often so great that their fragments have sometimes been confused.

Euripides would have found a freer scope for his peculiar gifts, and would have worked with more complete success, if he could have broken away from the trammels of tradition ; if he could have multiplied the actors at will, chosen his subject-matter where he would, altered the style of the costumes, and abolished the Chorus. Beautiful as his lyrics often are, they would charm still more as independent odes. But he could not thus emancipate himself, because Tragedy was a part of the Dionysiac worship, and the tradition which prescribed its type was also the sanction of its existence. It was needful that Tragedy should die before it could live again, the old name with a new form and a new spirit.

How Euripides was shackled.

In the Roman adaptation of the Greek New Comedy a novel feature was introduced, fraught with consequences more important than itself. The division into scenes and acts, following on the abolition of the Chorus, was not, in Roman practice, accompanied with free change of scene, or with liberty for the dramatist to suppose as long an interval of time between scenes as he might desire. But it prepared the way for deliverance from the thraldom of the "unities," a freedom which confers such an advantage on the modern theatre.

Roman modification of the Greek model.

After the Roman reproductions of Greek Comedy, a long period, fruitful in new influences, elapsed before the advent of
Romantic Drama, of which Shakespeare
is the greatest representative. In the Dark Ages,
the classical plays still found readers among the
learned, — chiefly in monasteries ; but there was
no theatre as a place of amusement. The popular
entertainers were not actors but story-tellers —
minstrels, troubadours, and the like. The very
words "Tragedy" and "Comedy" ceased to have
dramatic associations. Such stories as those in
the "Mirror for Magistrates" were called tragedies;
Dante could call his grave epic the "Divine Comedy." Stories in prose and verse, — sacred, taken
from Scripture, or concerning the Saints — secu-
lar, concerning deeds of chivalry or marvelous
adventure — were the delight of the Middle Age.
The entire range of such stories falls under the
word "Romance," which merely expresses the
group of languages, all sprung from that of
Rome, in which such stories were current. The
first meeting of Romance with its almost forgotten predecessor, Drama, was in the Mysteries
and Miracle Plays, from the twelfth century
onwards, — which had for their first object to
place sacred stories before the eyes of a laity
unable to read Latin. The Miracle Play dealt
with some portion of Scripture history, or with
the life of a Saint: the Mystery, with some part
of New Testament history which concerned a

Transition from Ancient to Modern Drama.

mysterious subject, such as the Incarnation or
the Atonement. The Morality was another step
towards drama ; — a play in which the characters
were personified virtues and vices, or such allegorical agents as Wealth, or Death. Yet one
step more was taken when the abstract virtues
and vices were replaced by men typical of them ;
as Aristeides might represent justice. And then
the circle of characters came to be enlarged so as
to include human life generally, as in John Hey-
wood's Interludes in Henry VIII.'s reign.

The regular drama was now at hand. The
first English comedy, "Ralph Roister Doister,"
was written by Nicholas Udall, before 1551. The
first English tragedy, "Gorboduc," by Sackville
and Norton, was acted in 1562, two years before
Shakespeare's birth. This new drama is called
the Romantic, in contradistinction to the Classical,
because Romance furnished it with most of its
material. But the ancient drama, revealed anew
by the Renaissance, gave the outlines of its form,
and strongly influenced its construction. There
was indeed a school of criticism, not extinct,
though defeated, in Shakespeare's time, which
contended for the strict observance of the ancient
unities in respect to time and place. Ben Jonson
combated it by arguing that the ancient drama
itself had been gradually developed, and that
moderns were entitled to carry the development
further, "instead," as he says, "of being tied to
those strict and regular forms which the niceness

of a few, who are nothing but form, would thrust upon us."

In recalling, however briefly, this course of progress from ancient to modern drama,

Attic Tragedy — its claim defined.

we are already warned against making an exaggerated claim for that unique and splendid phase of dramatic poetry — the earliest — which is known as Attic Tragedy. It is not the absolute measure, for all times and peoples, of what Tragedy should or can be. It does not furnish a norm by which Shakespeare or Goethe or Victor Hugo can be adequately tried. But in its own kind Attic Tragedy is supreme. It is the final outcome of the Greek genius in poetry; it has absorbed into itself elements of all that was best in the forms which went before it. It is also a perfect expression of the Athenian mind in the best age of Athens; that is, of the greatest national genius for literary art which history can show, seen at the moment of its highest excellence.

The whole history of classical Greek poetry was that of a natural growth. Epos ex-

Natural growth of Greek poetry.

presses one stage of the Hellenic development, Lyric poetry a second, Attic Drama a third. Each, in its own time and in its own way, represents an order of beliefs and feelings to which the poet gave, indeed, a clearer and more beautiful embodiment, but which was already pervading the Hellenic world of his age. Each, too, is addressed to hearers more directly than to

readers; its interpreter is the living voice of the
reciter, of the lyric singer, or of the actor. In the
literature of Rome, and of the modern world, it is
only the ruder phases of poetry, those of folk-song
or ballad, which exhibit such a relation to national
life. But Greek poetry preserved this relation so
long as creative force remained to it. The classification, Epic, Lyric, Dramatic, is itself a proof.
The general rules governing each of these forms
were gradually shaped by poets in response to the
needs of Hellenic audiences. The laws of Epos
were evolved by the conditions of a minstrel's
recitation at a banquet or on some public occasion. The laws of the Lyric were shaped by the
requirements of choral worship at Dorian festivals,
or by the usages of Aeolian society. The principal laws of Drama were determined by the Attic
ritual of Dionysus. And when these general
laws had been thus shaped, they were binding
on the poet; his original genius was to be shown
in his handling of the instrument prescribed to
him, not in devising new instruments of his own;
he could introduce new details, but the great outlines were fixed. His subject-matter decided the
form which he was to employ. The series of great
poets in any modern literature would illustrate
this by contrast. Take, for example, English
poetry from Spenser to Wordsworth; the literary
development can be traced, no doubt, to the
causes which connect it with the general intellectual progress of the nation, and with the social or

political influences of different periods ; but it is
not, in the direct Greek sense, a spontaneous and
continuous expression of national life ; and therefore it does not follow, in the Greek sense, the
course of a natural growth.

Hence there is no poetry of which it is so true
as of the Greek that it ought to be
studied in the historical order of its
development. Homer is the best preparation for Pindar ; Homer is again the
best aid, and Pindar no small aid, to the comprehension of the Attic drama. In the classical age the
whole bent of the Greek mind was retrospective.
Descending the stream of Greek poetry from its
source, we gradually learn to appreciate the feeling with which successive Greek poets looked
back upon the spiritual past of their race. It
would be a further aid to such appreciation, if it
were possible to restrict our field of view as it was
restricted for the Greeks themselves. But no
modern can strictly confine his thoughts within
the mental boundaries of ancient Greece; despite
all his efforts, disturbing cross-lights from later
ages will steal in, and color or obscure his vision of
that far-off world. The Attic drama, with its definite framework, its clear outlines, and its strong con-
centration, is the form of Greek poetry least liable
to these effects ; it is that which we can hope to see
most nearly from the Hellenic point of view. In
Tragedy, this is made possible for us by Aeschylus
and Sophocles ; in Comedy, by Aristophanes. The

The order of that growth should be followed in study.

spectacle offered by Euripides is, in itself, less purely Hellenic ; but if we only remember that, then we can enjoy without reserve the peculiar gift which his genius has bequeathed to the modern world, — a blending of Hellenic light, though that light is declining, with the incipient promise of Romance.

VIII

THE PERMANENT POWER OF GREEK POETRY

In a survey of Greek poetry, epic, lyric, and Relation of Greek poetry to Greek life. dramatic, we have seen how, in each successive phase, it was the voice of Greek life. The very word "literature" is fraught with associations which tend to obscure this fact. Writing was, indeed, the instrument by which the poems were preserved and transmitted. In the second half of the fifth century B. C. copies of the most popular works were diligently multiplied and widely circulated. But it belonged to the very essence of all the great poetry that it appealed to hearers rather than to readers. The Greeks of the classical age were eager listeners and talkers : they delighted in lively conversation and subtle discussion, but they were not great students of books. It was the interchange of living speech that sharpened their quick apprehension and gave elasticity to their intelligence. There is a striking passage in the Phaedrus of Plato which expresses the genuine Greek feeling on this subject. The written record of thought, Socrates says, is, taken by itself, an inanimate thing. There are two brothers, the spoken *logos* and the written *logos ;* but the first alone is true-born ; the second is illegitimate ; it does not inherit the full capacities of reason; if it is questioned, it remains dumb; if it is attacked, it can offer no defense. The spoken *logos*, indeed, alone is really existent; the written is a mere phantom of it. In the place where this remark occurs, it points to the difference between a barren Rhetoric and a fruitful Dialectic. But the remark itself is of still wider application. In every province of intellectual activity, and in that of poetry among the rest, the Greeks of the classical age demanded a living sympathy of mind with mind. What they felt in regard to the poet can be best understood by comparing it with the feeling which not they alone, but all people, have in regard to the orator and the preacher. The true orator, the great preacher, speaks out of the fulness of genuine conviction and emotion to the minds and hearts of those who hear him; through all variations of mood and tone, he keeps in mental touch with them. The excellence of the classical Greek poet was tried by the same test. No refinement or elaboration of art could sustain the poet through his ordeal, if he failed in truth to nature. False sentiment may pass muster in the study, but it is inevitably betrayed by its own unveracity when it is spoken aloud before listeners whose minds are sane, as those of the Greeks preëminently were; the hollow ring is detected; it offends; and the exemption of the best Greek poetry from false sentiment is a merit secured by the very conditions under which that poetry was produced.

The form of expression, again, was controlled by this tribunal of sound-minded hearers. A style might be novel and bold in any degree that the poet's faculty could reach; but at least it was required to have in it the pulse of life; it would be repugnant to his audience if they perceived the artificial outcome of mechanical formulas, a style which sought to impress or surprise by mere tricks of phrase, having no vital relation to his thought. When Aristophanes quotes such tricks of phrase, even from a poet so great in many ways as Euripides, we seem to catch an echo of Athenian laughter; we feel how strong and how sober was the control which the Athenian theatre exercised in this direction. When the work of the composer failed to be vital and sincere, this, the unpardonable fault, was described by the expressive word ψυχρός, *frigid.* The composition was then no longer a living thing, which spoke to the hearers, and elicited a response. It was stricken with the chill of death.

Thus the Greek poetry of the great age was not merely inspired by life; it was regulated by life; the instinct of the hearers was a restraint operating upon the poet, a safeguard against affectation or unreality. The freshness, the charm of nature, the immortal youth, which belong to such Greek poetry are due not simply to the qualities of the Greek mind, but also to this relation between the poet and his audience. This fact cannot be too much emphasized, for it at once constitutes an

essential difference between the best Greek poetry and such as has been produced under the conditions of a literary age, one of books and readers.
In a literary age the influence of criticism upon
poetry operates through the individual critic, who
either speaks for himself alone, or is the exponent
of a school or a coterie. Such criticism, working
on the sensitive temperament of a poet, is too apt
to check his spontaneity; on the other hand, it
does not necessarily help to keep him in accord
with nature, that is, with the first law of poetical
truth and beauty. But the Greek poet's spontaneity was in no way checked by his audience;
they only required that he should maintain a living relation with them. It is a familiar experience
that the collective impression of intelligent listeners, to a speech, let us say, or to a sermon, has a
critical value of a certain kind which can seldom
be claimed for the judgment of any single critic.
There is a certain magnetic sympathy, generated
by the mere presence of fellow-listeners, which
more or less influences each member of such a
company. He can scarcely avoid considering how
that to which he is listening is likely to affect
other minds beside his own. The very atmosphere of human companionship tends to preserve
the sanity of the individual judgment. In the
case of people with the unique gifts of the Greek
race, — their obedience to reason, and their instinct for beauty, — the critical value of the collective impression was exceptionally high. Their

poets were subject to a test which, while leaving them the largest freedom, also warned them, with unfailing accuracy, when they were in danger of going wrong.

Further, it should be remembered that poetry, orally delivered, not written for readers, had been from the earliest times the very basis of Greek education. The Greek genius had reached full maturity before written literature became important, and before literary prose had been developed. There is no more significant testimony of this fact than is afforded by the manner in which Greeks of the classical age conceived the office of the poet. They regarded him as primarily a teacher. Aristophanes frequently expresses this view of his own calling, and is a true interpreter of orthodox Greek sentiment when he enumerates the lessons which may be learned in various departments from the older poets. Aristotle was the first who formally asserted that the aim of poetry, as of all fine art, is to give noble pleasure, and that its didactic use is accidental. But the older conception held its ground, and often reappears in the later Greek literature. Strabo, in the Augustan age, can still describe poetry as an elementary philosophy, which instructs us — pleasurably, no doubt — in regard to character, emotion, action. With the same meaning, he observes that no one can be a good poet who is not first a good man. Plutarch gives still more forcible expression to the same

[marginal note: Old Greek view of the poet as a teacher — what it implies.]

sentiment: poetry, he says, is a kind of twilight, — a soft light in which truth is tempered with fiction, — to which the young are introduced in order that their eyes may be gradually prepared for the full sunshine of philosophy. In the Roman writers, too, this old Greek view can be traced, though sometimes blended with the Aristotelian, as when Horace insists equally on the *utile* and the *dulce;* and from the Roman world it passed on to the Renaissance. The prevalent view of the Elizabethan age, as given by Sir Philip Sidney in his " Apology for Poetry," was that the end of poetry is " delightful teaching." Dryden was something of a heretic when he ventured to say, " I am satisfied if " verse " cause delight ; for delight is the chief, if not the only, end of poesy." It may seem strange that the view of poetry as primarily didactic, a view which might be deemed prosaic, should have been that which was generally held by the Greeks, the most artistic of all races, in the age when their artistic faculties were at the best. But it is needful to distinguish between this view as it was held in Hellenistic or Roman times, and as it was held by the Greeks of an earlier period. What it really signifies, in its old Greek form, is that poetry was interwoven with the whole texture of Greek life. The voice of the poet was the voice from which the people had been accustomed, through long generations, to derive every thought that raised their minds above daily routine, and every sentiment that

came home to their hearts with living power.
When they spoke of the poet as a teacher, and of
poetry as didactic, this did not imply any indiffer-
ence to beauty and form, or to the delight which
such form gives ; it was simply a recognition of
poetry as the highest influence, intellectual and
spiritual, which they knew.   It was not merely a
recreation of their leisure, but a power pervading
and moulding their whole existence.   The ethical
aspect, to which they habitually gave prominence,
was in their conception inseparable from the artistic, and became thus prominent because, to
them, poetry was a thing so potent and so serious.
This was the sense in which the Greeks of the
classical age spoke of poetry as didactic ; it was,
in reality, quite different from the sense in which
the same view of it was enunciated by the literary
moralists of a later time, who regarded Greek poetry as a treasure-house of maxims or sentiments
wherewith to point their rules of conduct and to
fill their anthologies.   Between the two stands
Aristotle's doctrine that the end of poetry is to
give noble pleasure, — a doctrine, which, as we can
now see, was itself a testimony to the fact, of which
in his Poetics and his Rhetoric he implies his
consciousness, that the creative age of the Greek
genius was finished.

A broad line separates that age, in respect of
its poetical work, from every other.
Greek poetry
of the best age
— its distinc-
tion.   In no second instance has the world
seen the most perfect art of expression

joined to such direct sympathy with the living soul of the people whose mind was thus interpreted. The great types of Greek poetry, epic, lyric, dramatic, became permanent traditions; they passed on from one nation to another, receiving various modifications, while always preserving the traces, direct or indirect, of their origin; the Greek spirit, too, reappears now and again, though fitfully and partially, in later times; but the combination of form with spirit which distinguishes the classical poetry of Greece remains unique.

Of all the stages through which the Greek tradition passed, none is more instructive than the Alexandrian. It is so near to the great Hellenic age in time, it has so many links with it, and yet the difference is so profound. The best poetry of Greece had been nourished by two inspirations, working together for beauty, for natural freshness and vigor, for sincerity; these inspirations were religion and political freedom. The Alexandria of the third century B. C. had no longer the inspiration of the Hellenic religion. In the religion of Alexandria, the Oriental element, mingled with Hellenic forms and names, was already predominant, often in shapes which were not only non-Hellenic, but non-Aryan, being distinctly Semitic both in form and in origin. This tendency had begun, indeed, earlier; but it implied a fundamental change of thought and of feeling when cults such as that of Adonis came

to be publicly and generally practised by Greeks.
Then as to civic life, it was not merely in form of
government that the capital of the Ptolemies differed from the free cities of the elder Hellas.
We remember Aristotle's views as to the proper
limit of size for a city. "A city could not con-
sist," he says, "of ten men, nor, again, of one hundred thousand" (Eth. N. 9. 10). A city of one
hundred thousand (free) inhabitants would have
been, in Aristotle's estimate, no longer a civic
society, a πόλις, but something more unwieldy. It
has been computed that at the end of the Peloponnesian war the total free population of Athens was
less than seventy thousand. Aristophanes can
assume that his Athenian audience will seize each
of his innumerable allusions to fellow-citizens,
whom we may suppose to have been, in many
cases, of no public eminence, and who nevertheless were familiar to the mass of their fellow-citizens by their personal peculiarities, failings, or
merits. This compactness of social life was an
intellectual gain to poetry. But Alexandria in the
third century B. C. was like a huge modern city.
It had a population of about eight hundred thousand. Every country of the ancient world contributed its quota to that multitude. There was
a native Egyptian quarter, prolific in beggars by
day and burglars by night. There was a large
Jewish quarter, harboring chiefly men of business
or men of letters. Soldiers from Greece, Italy,
Sicily, and Asia were enrolled among the guards

of the Ptolemies. Merchants from the furthest
East brought the porcelain of China and the
choicest products of India to the marts of the
great capital. Literature, like art, was no longer
a public delight, prepared by citizens for citizens ;
it was now mainly the pleasure of princes and
millionaires, and was produced by men who might
be described as professional men of letters. The
Alexandrian age is the earliest that can be called,
in a modern sense, literary ; the earliest in which
a literary class catered for select, though numer-
ous, readers. The learned poets of Alexandria
wielded the classical Greek language with complete mastery of its vocabulary ; their models,
the classical Greek writers, were thoroughly familiar to them ; they had explored all the paths
of Greek mythology, even the most devious and
obscure. Yet, in reading Callimachus or Apollonius Rhodius we speedily become aware that the
difference between them and the older poets is
not merely one of degree, but, in respect to what
makes poetry vital, a difference of kind. They
are ingenious, elegant, copious ; their gift of expression is often brilliant ; but the thing which is
not there is the breath of life. Their work is the
work of the study, artificial, elaborate, charged
with allusions gathered by their wide reading,
embellished with words and phrases culled from
all the highways and by-ways of poetical diction ;
but if, in the great age of Greece, such poems had
been tried by the sound natural instinct of a

Greek audience, they would not have been saved
by their occasional beauties ; taken in the mass,
they would have been condemned as ψυχρά, frigid.

The Alexandrian age can show only one poet
who has a true affinity with the great
past of Greek song, and that is Theocritus. His rural idyls are no sham pastorals, but
true to the sights and sounds of his native Sicily.
The Sicilian sunshine is there, the shade of oak-
trees or pine, the " couch, softer than sleep,"
made by ferns or flowers ; the "music of water
falling from the high face of the rock," the ar-
butus shrubs, with their bright red berries, above
the sea-cliffs, whence the shepherds watch the
tunny-fishers on the sea below, while the sailors'
song floats up to them ; and if the form given to
the strains of shepherd and goatherd is such as
finished poetry demands, this is a very different
thing from the affectation of the mock pastoral,
as it existed, for instance, at the court of Louis
XIV. The modern love-songs of Greek shepherds
warrant the supposition that their ancient proto-
types commanded some elegance of expression ;
and whatever may be the degree in which Theocritus has idealized his Sicilian peasants, at any
rate we hear the voice and breathe the air of
nature. His twenty-first idyl is a dialogue between two old fishermen, who wake before day-
light in their wattled cabin on the Sicilian coast.
One of them tells the other a dream that he has
just had ; he had caught a golden fish, and had

Theocritus.

vowed that he would give up his hard calling. His comrade advises him to go on with his work, for dreams of gold will not feed him. Of this idyl Mr. Lang truly says, " There is nothing in Wordsworth more real, more full of the incommunicable sense of nature, rounding and softening the toilsome days of the aged and the poor. It is as true to nature as the statue of the naked fisherman in the Vatican. One cannot read these verses but the vision returns to one, of sandhills by the sea, of a low cabin roofed with grass, where fishing-rods of reed are leaning against the door, while the Mediterranean floats up her waves that fill the waste with sound. This nature, gray and still, seems in harmony with the wise content of old men whose days are waning on the limit of life, as they have all been spent by the desolate margin of the sea." But the idyls of Theocritus are not all rural ; and he too, when he handled epic material, had to write in the Alexandrian manner ; as in his hymn to the Dioscuri, and his two idyls on Heracles, the serpent-strangler and the lion-slayer. The general Alexandrian character is seen in the adaptation of the subjects to a small framework, the avoidance of the large epic style, the prettiness of detail given by a number of pictorial touches. It is a significant fact that Theocritus, the last genuinely inspired poet of Hellas, draws his true inspiration not from civic but from rural life, and is least Hellenic, in the old sense, just when he is most in accord with the taste of the great city in which he dwelt.

In the Alexandrian age, with all its close study and imitation of the classical models, nothing is more remarkable than the absence of any promise that the Hellenic spirit which animated those masterpieces was destined to have any abiding influence in the world. If that spirit was already so languid or almost dead in Greek-speaking men so familiar with its works, how could it be expected that aliens in blood and in language, aliens further removed from the great days of Greece not merely in time but in all the conditions of their lives, should prove more appreciative disciples, or more faithful guardians, of the Hellenic tradition? And yet it is true that the vital power of the Hellenic genius was not fully revealed, until, after suffering some temporary eclipse in the superficially Greek civilizations of Asia and Egypt, it emerged in a new quality, as a source of illumination to the literature and the art of Rome. Early Roman literature was indebted to Greece for the greater part of its material; but a more important debt was in respect to the forms and moulds of composition. The Latin language of the third century B. C. was already in full possession of the qualities which always remained distinctive of it; it was clear, strong, weighty, precise, a language made to be spoken in the imperative mood, a fitting interpreter of government and law. But it was not flexible or graceful, musical or rapid; it was not suited to express delicate shades of thought or

The Greek influence on Rome.

feeling; for literary purposes, it was, in comparison with Greek, a poor and rude idiom. The development of Latin into the language of Cicero and Virgil was gradually and laboriously accomplished under the constant influence of Greece. That finish of form, known as classical, which Roman writers share with Greek, was a lesson which Greece slowly impressed upon Rome. The Roman character was far too distinctive and too vigorous to be merged in any foreign influence. A peculiarity of the Roman mind was indeed its capacity to receive new impressions, and to assimilate foreign influences, without losing its own powerful individuality. On the other hand, a close and prolonged study of the Greek models could not end in a mere discipline of form; the beauty of the best Greek models depends too much on their vital spirit. Not only was the Roman imagination enriched, but the Roman intellect, through literary intercourse with the Greek, gradually acquired a flexibility and a plastic power which had not been among its original gifts. Through Roman literature the Greek influence was transmitted to later times in a shape which obscured, indeed, much of its charm, but which was also fitted to extend its empire, and to win an entrance for it in regions which would have been less accessible to a purer form of its manifestation.

In the earlier period of the Renaissance the scholars of Italy, where the revival had its chief seat, were engrossed with Latin literature; they

The Renais-
sance — pre-
dominantly
Latin.

regarded it as their Italian heritage, restored to them after long deprivation. Greek studies, though ardently pursued by a few, remained, on the whole, in the background. And it may be said that the general spirit of the classical revival continued to be Latin rather than Greek down to the latter part of the last century. Even where Greek scholarship was most cultivated, there was comparatively little sense of what is characteristic and distinctive

Hellenic
reaction of
18th century.

in the best Greek literature. This sense was developed, in the second half of the eighteenth century, chiefly through two agencies. One was the study of Greek art as advanced by such men as Winckelmann and Lessing, bringing with it the perception that the qualities characteristic of the best Greek art are also present in the best Greek literature. The other agency was the reaction against the conventional classicism, wearing a Latin garb, which had so long been in vogue. Minds insurgent against that tyranny turned with joyous relief to the elastic freedom of the Greek intellect, to the living charm of Greek poetry and Greek art. Goethe and Schiller are representatives of the new impulse. The great gain of the movement which then began was that, for the first time since the revival of letters, the Greek originals stood out distinct from the Latin copies; men acquired a truer sense of the Hellenic genius,

and the current of Hellenic influence upon modern life began to flow in a clear channel of its
own, no longer confused with the somewhat
turbid stream of Renaissance classicism.

Meanwhile, however, literature and art had ex-
perienced the influence of other forces, Influences
acting in very different ways ; and with competing
these forces the Hellenic influence had Hellenic.
to reckon. One of these was the product of mediaeval Catholicism, which had given art a
new genius. A new world of beauty had Mediaeval art.
arisen, even more different from the pagan world
than the Empire of the twelfth century was different from that of the first. Greek art had sprung
from a free, cheerful life, open to all the bright
impressions of external nature, a life warmed by
frank human sympathies, and lit up with fancy
controlled by reason. The lawgivers of mediaeval
art were men withdrawn from communion with
the outward world by the rapture of a devotion
at once half-mystic and intensely real ; instead of
flexible intelligence, they had religious passion ;
instead of the Greek's clear and steady outlook
upon the facts of humanity, they had a faith which
transfigured the actual world, which adjusted every
relation of life by its own canons, which indeed
made itself the standard by which the impressions
of the senses were to be judged. The Greek artist, even in portraying passion, was mindful of bal-
ance, and placed certain limits on the expression
of individual character ; the mediaeval artist strove

before all things to express the intensity of the
individual soul.   In poetry Dante is the great exponent of this spirit, and mediaeval Catholicism
deeply colored the sentiment of all the literature
known by the general name of Romantic.

Classical and
Romantic   In Goethe's younger days the conflict
Schools.
between the Classical and the Romantic
schools raged fiercely.   The interlude of Helena,
which forms the third act in the sec-
Goethe.
ond part of " Faust," was the work of his
old age (1830).   Faust's nature is to be elevated
and purified by developing in him the sense of
beauty ; Helena represents the classical, but especially the Greek, element in art and literature ;
and when Faust at last wins her, their union
typifies the reconciliation of the Romantic with
the Classical.   Goethe himself, as one of his critics says, dated a new life, a complete mental re-
generation, from the time when he first seized
the true spirit of the ancient masters.   In his
own words, speaking of Greek art and literature :
" Clearness of vision, cheerfulness of acceptance,
easy grace of expression, are the qualities which
delight us ; and now, when we affirm that we find
all these in the genuine Grecian works, achieved
in the noblest material, the best-proportioned form,
with certainty and completeness of execution, we
shall be understood if we always refer to them
as a basis and a standard.   Let each one be a
Grecian in his own way ; but let him *be* one."   In
the allegorical strain which pervades the Helena,

Goethe has not failed to mark that, while the Hellenic idea of beauty is supreme, the Romantic element has also enriched modern life. The gifts are not all from one side. The symmetry, the clear outlines, the cheerful repose of Classical art, are wedded to the sentiment, passion, and variety of the Romantic. The great German poet felt, and has expressed with wonderful subtlety, the truth that no modern can absolutely dissociate the Hellenic influence from the others which have contributed to shape modern life; no one can now be a pure Hellene, nor, if he could, would it be desirable; but every one should recognize the special elements with which the Hellenic ideal can ennoble and chasten the modern spirit, and these he should by all means cultivate. To do so successfully is to educate one's sense of beauty; and to do that aright is to raise and purify one's whole nature.

This great lesson, taught half-mystically in the second part of "Faust," is apt to be obscured by a contrast much deeper than any that ever existed between the Romantic and the Classical schools, — one of which Goethe took little account, since it did not much concern him, — the contrast between Hellenism and Hebraism. As Mr. Matthew Arnold says in "Culture and Anarchy," the governing idea of Hellenism is spontaneity of consciousness; that of Hebraism is strictness of conscience. Both seek, in the Hebrew Apostle's words, to make

us partakers of the divine nature ; but Hellenism
seeks to do this through the reason, by making
us see things as they are ; Hebraism insists rather
on conduct and obedience. The Renaissance was
a movement away from mediaeval Catholicism in
the direction of Hellenism ; the Reformation was
a movement in the direction of Hebraism. In
countries where the Reformation took strongest
hold, and, owing to the qualities of our race, more
especially in England, the intellectual influence
of the Renaissance was crossed, and for a time
checked, by the Hebraizing tendency. The Puritan conception of righteousness, with all its moral
nobleness, was at that moment adverse to the ac-
quisition of the best things which the Hellenic influence had to bestow ; and in this sense it could
be said, with a melancholy truth, that the English
" entered the prison of Puritanism, and had the
key turned upon their spirit there for two hundred years."

But though there is a profound difference, there
is no necessary antagonism, between the
ideal broadly described as Hebraic, and
the permanent, the essential, parts of
Hellenism.   The Greek influence has acted upon
modern life and literature even more widely as a
pervading and quickening spirit than as an exemplar of form ; and it has shown itself capable of
coöperating, in this subtle manner, with various
alien forces, so as neither to lose its own distinction nor to infringe upon theirs.

The Greek
element
in alliance
with others.

In respect to Hebraism, Milton illustrates this. By temperament no less than creed, Milton was a Puritan of the higher type.

Milton.

He had an austere belief in his own mission to be for England a prophet, a mouthpiece of moral teaching and moral warning, just as he believed, and said, that the English nation was, in the Hebrew sense, a chosen people. He was also steeped in classical culture. In an age of classicism which, outside of Italy, was usually superficial, he was the first Englishman who had joined a thorough appreciation of the classical literature (especially Latin) to a first-rate original genius for poetry. I do not forget Ben Jonson, at once scholar and poet; but in neither quality was he Milton's equal. How, then, is the Hellenic influence seen in Milton? It cannot be said to have determined the pervading spirit of his work; that is rather Hebraic, or, when it is not Hebraic, Latin. The "Lycidas," for instance, is a pastoral elegy on the Alexandrian model; but how strangely is the temper of the Greek original changed when the English poet blazes forth in Puritan indignation against the corruptions of the Church! The poet himself shows his consciousness of this in reverting from the digression to his theme: —

> Return, Alpheus, the dread voice is past
> That shrunk thy streams — return, Sicilian Muse!

The "Samson Agonistes" has the form of a Greek drama, but its inspiration, like its subject, is far more Hebraic than Hellenic; it concerns

the mysterious dealing of Jehovah with his servant; it is full of questionings and strivings like
those of Job, followed by such a triumph as
rings through the song of Miriam or of Deborah.
Yet no one familiar with the best Greek poetry
can read Milton without feeling what its influence has contributed to his genius; it has
helped to give him his lofty self-restraint and his
serenity.

Another modern poet, who illustrates the co-
operation of the Greek influence with
Keats.   foreign influences, is Keats.   Unlike
Milton, Keats knew Greek literature only through
such scraps as he might find in classical diction-
aries, or, at most, through translation, as he knew
Homer through Chapman.   His grasp of Hellenic
things unavoidably lacks that sureness which is
found, for instance, in Landor, who, besides being
much of a Greek in feeling, had also an intimate
familiarity with Greek literature; on the other
hand, Keats had a native sympathy with the
spirit of Greek mythology; and even a Landor
could not achieve what Keats sometimes reaches
by flashes of insight.   The Greek element is,
however, only one of those which are present
in the poetry of Keats.   The romantic element
was not less vital in it; "St. Agnes' Eve" is not
less characteristic than the "Ode on a Grecian
Urn."   And his manner, even in treating Greek
subjects, was not Greek, except occasionally, and
for brief spaces.   His style had not the harmo-

nious and lucid simplicity of the best Greek style, which gives clear outlines to the central thought, dispensing with all ornament which might confuse or obscure it. Keats, like the Elizabethan poets, delighted in a luxuriance of decorative detail; his style is essentially romantic. In "Hyperion," for instance, the description of the god's palace,

> Bastion'd with pyramids of glowing gold,
> And touch'd with shade of bronzèd obelisks,

is throughout rather romantic in its splendors and its mystery than truly Hellenic. So also is this passage of "Endymion," beautiful in itself, but charged with imagery of an Elizabethan type, and lacking Hellenic simplicity : —

> As when, upon a trancèd summer night,
> Those green-robed senators of mighty woods,
> Tall oaks, branch-charmèd by the earnest stars,
> Dream, and so dream all night without a stir.

But in one quality of his genius Keats was truly a Greek, — namely, in his vivid, spontaneous sympathy with the life of external nature. Take, for example, his "Ode to a Nightingale ;" there we see the joy in nature for nature's own sake, penetrated by a feeling which is truly Hellenic ; not with the feeling of Shelley, that the visible world is but the veil of the unseen. Like a Greek, too, Keats loved to embody the powers of nature in human shapes of more than human loveliness, — unlike Wordsworth, to whom the influences of nature were emanations, not per-

sons, and whose joy in nature was also inseparable from those aspirations of his own mind which
he read into the scenes around him : —

> The clouds that gather round the setting sun
>   Do take a sober coloring from an eye
>   That hath kept watch o'er man's mortality:
> Another race hath been, and other palms are won.

The natural affinity of Keats with the Greek
mind is curiously illustrated by a letter to a
friend in which he argues against distrust of
the imagination as a guide to truth, saying, in
effect, that, when a beautiful vision rises before
the imagination, it is the imperfect reflex of a
divine prototype, which will be seen hereafter.
Keats had not read Plato, and yet here is the
tendency which received a more scientific expression in the theory of ideas.   When the poetry
of Keats was described as "the wail and remon-
strance of a disinherited paganism," the criticism
was singularly unjust.   A strain of imaginative
regret there indeed is in him, when he thinks
of what has gone out of the world with the inspirations of the ancient poetry : —

> Glory and loveliness have passed away.

But his regret was for the beauty, not for the
paganism ; and no one felt more finely the sense
in which the spiritual existence of that beauty has
been prolonged : —

> Heard melodies are sweet, but those unheard
>   Are sweeter ; therefore, ye soft pipes, play on ;
> Not to the sensual ear, but, more endear'd,
>   Pipe to the spirit ditties of no tone.

Other poets there have been, and are, who have consciously sought, and sometimes with exquisite results, to blend the Hellenic grace with a romantic coloring; as in Dante Gabriel Rossetti's sonnets on Greek subjects the language has a Greek clearness, lightness, and finish, while the spirit is rather that of the Italian Middle Age: or as Mr. William Morris clothes Greek stories in a mediaeval garb. Thus his " Jason " derives a peculiar charm from the mediaeval traits. When the Argonaut heroes move through the streets of Iolcos to embark, bells are ringing in the town, and ladies shower roses

> From windows glorious with the well-wrought hem
> Of many a purple cloth.

It is as if the poet were singing in the latter part of the Middle Age, when its enchantments were about to pass away before a clearer illumination: like the wreaths on the helmets of the Argonauts, the poet's fancies seem

> wet
> With beaded dew of the scarce-vanished night.

The distinction of such poetical work is the use of romance to bring Hellenism into relief; the inner contrasts between the romantic and the Hellenic spirit are rather hinted than expressed.

But the deepest and largest influence of Greece is not to be sought in the modern poetry which treats Greek subjects and imitates Greek form; that influence works more characteristically when, having been received into the modern mind, it acts by suggestion and inspiration, breathing a grace and a power of its own into material and form of a different origin : —

> totamque infusa per artus
> Mens agitat molem, et magno se in corpore miscet.

This influence has been all-pervading in modern life, in modern literature and art.

Yet those who most appreciate the true value Value of Hellenism for us; of Hellenism will never claim for it that, by itself, it can suffice for the needs of modern humanity. In the intellectual province its value is not only permanent, but unique; it has furnished models of excellence which can never be superseded ; by its spirit, it supplies a medicine for diseases of the modern mind, a corrective for aberrations of modern taste, a discipline, no less than a delight, for the modern imagination ; since that obedience to reason which it exacts is also a return to the most gracious activities of life and nature.   Of such a power, we may truly say,

> it will never
> Pass into nothingness, but still will keep
> A bower of quiet for us, and a sleep
> Full of sweet dreams and health and quiet breathing.

But in the province of religion and morals Hellenism alone is not sufficing. Greek and the limit thereto. polytheism, even as ennobled by the great poets, was incapable of generating religious conceptions which could satisfy the mind and

heart, or of furnishing an adequate rule for the
conduct of life. These must be sought from another source.

Yet there is no inherent conflict between true
Hellenism and spiritualized Hebraism, Healthy char-
that Hebraism which has passed into acter of the
best Greek
Christianity. Such a notion could be work.
entertained only where the apprehension of Hellenism itself was superficial or defective. There
has, indeed, been some poetry in which the direct
imitation of Greek form has been associated with
unhealthy tendencies; there have been transient
vagaries of modern fashion which have seemed to
assume that Hellenism is to be found, as has been
neatly said, in eccentricity tinged with vice. But
the distinctive quality of the best Greek poetry
and art, that by which it has lived and will live, is
the faculty of rising from the earth, from a soil
which nourishes weeds along with flowers, into a
clearer air. " The divine," says Plato in the
Phaedrus, " is beauty, wisdom, goodness, and the
like; by these the wing of the soul is nourished, and grows apace; but when fed upon evil
and foulness and the like, wastes and falls away."
Greek poetry, in its noblest forms, was indeed the
πτεροῦ δύναμις, " the power of the wing," for the
human soul; the visions to which it soared were
such as that described in the Phaedrus, where
beauty is beheld dwelling with σωφροσύνη, modesty,
in a holy place, as in a shrine; and in the emotion
which this divine beauty stirs, love is blended with

reverent adoration. The spirit of the highest
Greek poetry, as of the best Greek art, is essentially pure ; to conceive it as necessarily entangled
with the baser elements of paganism is to con-
found the accidents with the essence; the accidents have passed away ; the essence is imperishable. Nor is it purity alone that can be claimed
for such Greek poetry ; it is capable of acting as
an intellectual tonic, and of bracing us for the
battle of life. There is truth in the words with
which Mr. Gladstone concludes his "Studies on
Homer:" —

"To pass from the study of Homer to the business of the world is to step out of a palace of
enchantment into the cold, gray light of a polar
day. But the spells in which this enchanter
deals have no affinity with that drug from Egypt
which drowns the spirit in effeminate indiffer-
ence ; rather they are like the φάρμακον ἐσθλόν, the
remedial specific, which, freshening the understanding by contact with the truth and strength
of nature, should both improve its vigilance against
deceit and danger, and increase its vigor and reso-
lution for the discharge of duty."

A like tribute might be paid, with not less
justice, to the classical Greek poetry as a whole.
True to Aristotle's principle for art, this poetry
deals with the universal, — with those elements of
human character and life which are not transient
or abnormal, but of interest for every age and
every land. What Mr. Lowell said of the ancient

classical literature generally applies especially to
the Greek: "It is as contemporary with to-day
as with the ears it first enraptured; for it appeals not to the man of then or now, but to the
entire round of human nature itself. . . . We
know not whither other studies will lead us, especially if dissociated from this; we do know to
what summits, far above our lower region of
turmoil, this has led, and what the many-sided
outlook thence."

The claims of classical Greek poetry to a permanent hold upon the attention of the Conclusion:
civilized world are of two kinds, intrin- the enduring claims of
sic and historical. Viewed in regard to Greek poetry.
its intrinsic qualities, this poetry is the creation
of a people in whom the gifts of the artists were
more harmoniously united than in any other race;
it bears the impress of their mind in the perfection of its form; it is also the spontaneous and
profoundly suggestive expression of their life and
thought. Viewed historically, this poetry is the
fountain-head of poetical tradition in Europe; it
has supplied the typical standards of form, it has
also furnished a varied wealth of material and
illustration; even where it has not given a direct
model, it has operated by the subtle diffusion of
an animating spirit; it has become blended with
various other influences of later origin, and to
every such alliance it has contributed some intellectual distinction which no other element could
have supplied. So far from being adverse to

those religious and ethical influences which are
beyond the compass of its own gift to modern
life, it is, rightly understood, in concord with
them, inasmuch as it tends to elevate and to
refine the human spirit by the contemplation of
beauty in its noblest and purest form.   On the
high places of Greek literature, those who are
worn with the troubles or disturbed by the mental
maladies of modern civilization can breathe an
atmosphere which, like that of Greece itself, has
the freshness of the mountains and the sea.   But
the loneliness of Oeta or Cithaeron is not there;
we have around us, on those summits, also the
cheerful sympathies of human life, the pleasant
greetings of the kindly human voice.   The great
poets of ancient Hellas recall to one's mind the
words in which Aeschylus described the kinsmen
of Niobe who worshiped their ancestral deity on
the mountain-heights of Mysia : —

> the seed of gods,
> Men near to Zeus; for whom on Ida burns,
> High in clear air, the altar of their Sire,
> Nor hath their race yet lost the blood divine.

Humanity cannot afford to lose out of its in-
heritance any part of the best work which has
been done for it in the past.   All that is most
beautiful and most instructive in Greek achievement is our permanent possession; one which
can be enjoyed without detriment to those other
studies which modern life demands; one which
no lapse of time can make obsolete, and which

no multiplication of modern interests can make superfluous. Each successive generation must learn from ancient Greece that which can be taught by her alone; and to assist, however little, in the transmission of her message is the best reward of a student.

INDEX.

Gods, the Homeric, 23, 70.
Goethe, 238.
Gothic Architecture, 29.
Graces, the, invocation to, by
Pindar, 147.
Graioi, 12.
Greek compared with Sanskrit,
21.
Greek monarchy, Aristotle on,
17.
Greek shepherds, love-songs of,
232.
Greeks, distinction of, among
Indo-Europeans, 27.
Gymnopaedia, festival of, 116.

Hebraism and Hellenism, con-
trast between, 239, 240.
Hector, 58.
Hellenic characteristics, 15.
Hellenic migrations, the, 12.
Hellenic reaction in 18th cen-
tury, 236.
Hellenism and Hebraism, con-
trast between, 239, 240.
Heracles, 153, 154.
Heracles, shield of, of Hesiod,
90.
Herodotus, 164.
Hesiod, rival of Homer, 79; poems of, 79; date of, 79; Theogony of, 88, 89; style of, compared with the Homeric, 91;
as a teacher, 92; literary interest of, 93.
Hexameter, character of, 97.
Homeric language, 21.
Homeric nobleness and rapidity, 56; use of direct speech,
61; simile, 61.
Homeric plainness of thought
and style, 54, 55.
Homeric poems, probable origin
of, 14; as a revelation of the
Greek faculties, 24; form of,
53; position of women in, 72;
characteristics of women in,
76; general character of, 78;
poetical art in, 78; style of,
compared with the Hesiodic,
91.

Iambic poetry, 103; obscurity of
its origin, 104; general character of, 106; compared with
elegiac, 106; illustration from
Solon, 107; kinship with elegiac, 107; why classed as lyric,
108.
Iambic satire, 105.
Ibycus, 119; characteristics of
his poetry, 119.
Iliad, the, religion in, 15; climax
of, 58; use of simile in, 62; resemblance between the Odyssey and, 64; differences between the Odyssey and, 64;
dramatic force of, 67.
Ionian colonies, civilization in
the, 95.

Jonson, Ben, 217.

Keats, 242; his relation to Greek
poetry, 242, 243.
Knowledge, Greek desire for, 20.

Landor, 242.
Language, Homeric, 21.
Lesbos, cultivation of music at,
110; school of citharodes at,
111, 158.
Lessing, 236.
"Limping" iambic verse or sca-
zon, 105.
Lore, magical, in the Odyssey,
68.
Lyre, invocation to, 146.
Lyric poetry, Greek, 94; period
of, 109; causes of its decline,
123.

Magical lore, in the Odyssey, 68.
Martial elegies, 99.
Maxims of Hesiod, 87.
Mediaeval art, 237.
Melancholy, Greek, 20.
Melic poetry, 108.
Menelaus, 77.
Migrations, Hellenic, 12.
Milton, quoted, 57; his apprecia-
tion of classical literature, 241.
Mimnermus, 99.